SERVANT WARFARE

SERVANT WARFARE

How Kindness Conquers
Spiritual Darkness

STEVE SJOGREN

Servant Publications
Ann Arbor, Michigan

Vine Books is an imprint of Servant Publications especially designed to serve evangelical Christians.

Excerpt from *What's Gone Wrong with the Harvest?*, by James Engel and Wilbert Norton, © 1975 by The Zondervan Corporation, was used by permission of Zondervan Publishing House.

Some of the illustrations in this book are true to life and are included with the permission of the persons involved. In other cases, names and identifying details have been changed to protect the privacy of those involved. All other illustrations are composites of real situations, and any resemblance to people living or dead is coincidental.

Published by Servant Publications
P.O. Box 8617
Ann Arbor, Michigan 48107

96 97 98 99 00 10 9 8 7 6 5 4 3 2 1

Printed in the United States of America
ISBN 0-89283-964-3

LIBRARY OF CONGRESS CATALOGING-IN-PUBLICATION DATA

Sjogren, Steve.
    Servant warfare : how kindness conquers spiritual darkness / Steve Sjogren.
      p. cm.
    Includes bibliographical references
    ISBN 0-89283-964-3
    1. Service (Theology) 2. Spiritual warfare. 3. Kindness—Religious aspects—
Christianity. 4. Christian life—Pentecostal authorsl. I. Title.
BT738.4.S55 1996
235'.4—dc20   96-22396
                                                      CIP

DEDICATION

To Alfild and Kyrre Kolvik.
You persevered in servant warfare for me
and that has made all the difference in my
life. Takk for alt!

Contents

ACKNOWLEDGMENTS

Thanks to my local editorial readers, Pam Fields, Mary Beshear, and my lovely wife Janie Sjogren. You three kept me on track and away from pushing the "I quit" button.

Thank you, Mary Ann Purmort and Greg Kazanian, for consistently praying for me. You both continue to be great gifts from God to me.

Thanks to my editor, Liz Heaney, for learning to actually understand how my mind works (a scary thought) and coaching me through the twists and turns of this book.

Thanks to Chuck Mancini for gathering information on the outreach projects for the appendix. You are a faithful friend.

Karen Andrea, you were wonderful at gathering research information for this book.

Thank you, Dave Nixon, for the language help. I'm glad it's not Greek to you.

INTRODUCTION

Rule #1: Don't sweat the small stuff.
Rule #2: It's all small stuff.
— **Dr. Michael Mantell** —

IN THE 1970S, COMEDIAN STEVE MARTIN became famous for appearing on stage with a fake arrow stuck in his head and commenting, "Boy, do I have a headache!" At some point later in his act he'd lose the arrow and say, "I think I know why I had a headache. There was an arrow stuck in my head!" With the audience roaring at the humor of his understatement Martin would comment, "You know, it's amazing how a small thing can make you feel a lot better."

Today it seems that many overlook the power of a small thing. For years I valued only the biggest, fastest, largest, and strongest within the ranks of Christianity. I didn't even notice the small, menial, and lowly. But Jesus used these more subtle forms to communicate his Good News. Like Steve Martin removing the arrow, I have begun to see that it's the small things in life that make the biggest difference. In fact, small things done with great love can change the world.

As you read this book, I hope that the way you think about spiritual darkness and your part in dealing with it will change. When we connect *spiritual warfare* to *serving* we begin to change our view of this traditionally scary topic.

In *Conspiracy of Kindness* I wrote that successful evangelism is within our reach as we use the power of God's kindness to open doors to the hearts of our community. I believe that same power is equally powerful in dismantling powers of darkness.

Over the past ten years Vineyard Community Church has served its way into the hearts of the people of Cincinnati. This past year over 180,000 residents were touched with some type of kindness project. I believe the Vineyard congregation's growth from thirty to three thousand members has occurred in large part because average followers of Jesus Christ have brought light to darkened lives with the simple power of his kindness.

I love the church of Jesus Christ, and I long to see it effectively influencing the world with the love of God. I'm not out to criticize other approaches to spiritual warfare; in fact, I applaud and encourage anyone who is trying to change the world with any biblical approach. My intention isn't to teach *the* angle, but rather to demonstrate a less obvious angle on how to deal with the powers of darkness according to scripture and my experience.

If you'd like to be linked by computer to a growing number of churches who are using kindness as an approach to spiritual warfare, send me your dedicated fax number for a free subscription to "se-mail" on our fax line at (513) 671-2041. For up-to-date project ideas, training opportunities, materials, and connections to other churches serving their community, check out our web site on the Internet at http://www.kindness.com/vineyard.

You can read this book on your own or study it in a group by using the questions at the end of each chapter. I call these "pair and share" questions in hopes that in the context of your small group, members can break into groups of two or three to discuss individual responses to the topics of each chapter.

We must work the works of Him who sent Me, as long as it is day; night is coming when no man can work.　　　John 9:4, NASB

THE FORGOTTEN
WEAPON

We forget three-fourth of ourselves
to be like other people.
— Arthur Schopenhauer —

Admittedly, we looked a bit odd. It isn't every day that some-one offers to clean the restrooms of a retail carpet store for free. I'm used to surprising people when I walk into their business wearing yellow gloves and carrying a toilet cleaning kit. But even I was taken aback by the response of the store manager this day.

I said, "We're Christians and we'd like to clean your toilets to show you God's love in a practical way." Looking stunned, she answered in a high-pitched voice, "You're what?"

"As Christians we believe it's better to give than to receive. We would rather serve than be served. We'd like to serve you by clean-ing."

I think she overreacted with her response: "You know, I have a good mind to call the cops on you. Why don't you get out of my store—now!"

In spite of her harsh answer, I couldn't help but smile a bit as I imagined being handcuffed with my yellow gloves on and being hauled into jail—for cleaning without a license!

Something in her tone led me to believe God was moving in her heart, so I wasn't surprised when she fired back a moment later, "Well, if it makes you feel good to clean our toilets, then go for it."

We made quick work of the restrooms and I stopped by on the way out the door to let her know we were done. I didn't expect her to thank us, but I was surprised when she snapped, "Before you leave, I want to talk to you." As I sat waiting for her to finish with a customer, I felt like an errant child awaiting discipline from the school principal. When she sat down I could see in her eyes she had experienced some above-average levels of pain in life.

"You guys are from that church down the street, aren't you?" By her tone I suspected we had done something to offend her so I said, "Yes, that's us. Did we do something wrong?"

◆◆◆

Small things done with great love
can change the world.

◆◆◆

Suddenly she did an about-face from anger to openness. "You know, I'm only twenty-nine years old, but I've managed to already thoroughly mess up my life. I've been addicted to alcohol and cocaine. I've had a child, though I've never been married. I'm in a dead-end job. My life seems shattered like a big bag of broken glass. As you were cleaning our toilets a question popped into my mind: *Would an addicted, messed-up person like me fit in at your church?*"

I was reeling over the rapid change of heart I had just seen and was unprepared for the surprise quiz she'd just thrown at me. I answered her candidly: "You would absolutely fit in at our church! And if you didn't feel comfortable, we'd start a new one just for addicted carpet-store managers!"

I walked out of the store shaking my head at what I'd just witnessed. This woman had probably spent years outside the church critically watching Christians, but never once thought the message of Christ had anything to offer her. Before my eyes, in a matter of minutes, God's love became real to her for the first time.

◆◆◆

Most Christians have not recognized kindness
as a useful weapon of spiritual warfare.

◆◆◆

This is an example of what I call "servant warfare"—that is, *using the power of kindness to penetrate the spiritually darkened hearts of people with the love of God.* With this simple approach to battling darkness, virtually all of us who follow Christ can break the grip of darkness around us. Most Christians, however, have not recognized kindness as a useful weapon of spiritual warfare.

KINDNESS AND SPIRITUAL WARFARE

Pretend for a minute that you're taking an ink blot test, and the words SPIRITUAL WARFARE flash before your eyes. What images would come to your mind? If you've rubbed shoulders with those in the Body of Christ for awhile, you've probably developed some common definitions of spiritual warfare. While there are many models for doing spiritual warfare, not all of them are easily attainable.

For example, some would picture the **prayer closet** approach: a white-haired saint faithfully "standing in the gap" for hours on end in the privacy of her intimate discourse with God. After years of faithfully developing her prayer skills she is able to plumb the depths of intercession on behalf of those in darkness. Prayer warriors like her pack great spiritual power, but their model for doing spiritual warfare is unattainable for most of us. Possibly one or two of these power house prayer warriors ushered you into Christ through faithful praying.

In contrast to this some would envision spiritual warfare as the actions of a **revivalist preacher** strutting about on a stage. Though something spiritual is taking place, few present can relate to the approach to ministry they see. The preacher's volume is far louder than necessary, and he dresses to the nines, wearing expensive clothes, a gold watch, and pinkie rings. But his most unusual characteristic is his ability to add an extra syllable to any word in the English language as he prays: "In the name-uh of-uh Jesus-uh, I rebuke-uh..." To first-timers his ways seem odd, but the veterans are convinced that everything about the evening is evidence that God is breaking the powers of darkness.

Some associate spiritual warfare with **massive rallies** where thousands of Christians in a city converge to pray in focused unity. These rallies may draw crowds of up to fifty thousand to pray in earnest. The only problem with this model is the huge logistical challenge of gathering so many people.

Others see warfare as **identifying and naming the powers** that rule over a city or region, then coming against them specifically and binding them in the name of the Lord. Christians who practice this form of warfare consider it mandatory that evil be taken on with great fervor. They are convinced that taking a strong-arm approach is the best way to deal with the powers of darkness.

All these models of spiritual warfare are valid and are, in my experience, at least somewhat effective. However, they all have one problem: *They're too expensive!* The average Christian can't afford what these approaches cost in terms of time, experience, gifting, or courage. Not many of us are prayer warriors or revival preachers or fervent intercessors. But that's OK; there's another option.

EXPANDING YOUR ARSENAL

I've discovered that we can effectively battle darkness without significantly changing our current patterns of living. In recent years I have expanded my spiritual warfare arsenal to include a powerful weapon that has been all but overlooked in the church today. It's the practical, non-threatening weapon that penetrated the defenses of the skeptical carpet store manager: *kindness!* Whether you recognize it or not, the kindness that already resides in you is a powerful tool for changing the spiritual state of things in your world.

I have often made the mistake of thinking that the words *new* and *improved* necessarily belong together. Perhaps you've had occasion to test a new product that promised an easier way of doing things, only to discover that the old, simpler approach worked better. That wisdom proves true in the spiritual realm as well as the physical one.

My dad had a friend who served in the Marines as a sniper during the Vietnam war in the early 1960s. Earl's job, plainly stated, was to sneak up on enemy troops and shoot them. He was trained to use a high-powered rifle with a special scope that could pick off the enemy from several hundred yards. After some months of training he was adequate at handling his weapon, but the rifle just didn't feel comfortable. Earl was raised in the Ozark region of southern Missouri where he developed skill in using homemade slingshots. As a kid he had hunted with slingshots and had bagged many game animals with his homemade weapons. He'd spent every day of his childhood summers exploring the woods near him with a slingshot almost constantly in his back pocket.

One day while out on patrol in the jungle of Vietnam, Earl thought, "I could do better with the weapon I began with back in Missouri!" On his own, without the permission of his superior officer, Earl gathered surgical rubber, some pipe, and ball bearings and assembled an Ozark-style slingshot. With a little practice he was able to hit a target accurately with great force. The best thing about his new weapon was its almost complete silence. While he was grateful for the technology available in the scoped rifle, he decided to go with the approach that worked best for him. His commanding officer was stunned to hear of this unorthodox approach to warfare, but no one could argue with his results. At the end of his duty Earl received an award of merit for his ingenuity!

If Christians are to make progress in spiritual warfare, I think we need to see an army of Earls raised up who are willing to move in the power of the Holy Spirit and be themselves in Christ at the same time. Earl may have been out of step with standard procedures of his day, but he had the honesty and common sense to use what worked for him.

Most of us can't relate to the complex or intense approaches to warfare that currently abound in the church and unfortunately don't see ourselves as soldiers sent by God to battle darkness in an active way. The conclusion for most is, "Darkness is real, but I can't do much to change it, so why even worry about it?"

The good news is that we all have a perfect weapon for battling darkness right in our back pockets. What we need is a little encouragement simply to be who we are in Christ and to use what we already have at our disposal. The power of kindness resides in every follower of Christ. When we learn to wield it, we change the world.

I became convinced of this truth when I attended a healing conference some years ago. As part of the prayer team I was asked to investigate a commotion that was taking place in a corner of the room. As I walked through the crowd watching the ruckus I heard one lady say, "It's OK, the ones praying for the guy are pastors." It was an odd sight: A man lay on the carpet with his back bowed so that only his head and heels touched the ground. Standing over him were three pastors, two trying to hold him down while the third waved his Bible and prayed loudly. Clearly they were not making progress, so when I offered to help they gladly handed the man off to me and offered to do anything they could to help.

I explained that I was no expert in these kinds of settings, but I would give it a shot. My first idea was to get the man a cup of water. The pastors asked, "How is that going to help free him from the power of darkness that's gripping him?"

"After all of the intense groaning he's been through," I answered, "his mouth must be dry, so let's help him out."

After this man had been touched by my practical care, he trusted me enough to let down his defenses. Instead of opposing the aggressive approach that had been coming his way, he opened his heart and let me lead him in a prayer. Within a few minutes the bondage he had been in was broken and his body relaxed.

The pastors were curious about what they'd just seen and asked, "What was that all about? We were using the authority of the Lord, so why didn't we get results?"

"Well, sometimes God's authority comes in small, quiet ways," I said. "You just need to expand your arsenal a little."

Pair and Share Questions

1. What models or images of spiritual warfare have you encountered?

2. Do you see any problems with these models for the average Christian who wants to use them?

3. In what ways do you see these models as costly?

4. Do you consider yourself a "prayer warrior"?

   If yes, what price have you paid to become one?

   If no, what has kept you from becoming one?

5. Consider the definition given of servant warfare: *using the power of kindness to penetrate the spiritually darkened hearts of people with the love of God.*

What is the tool mentioned here?

What is the function of that tool?

What is the ultimate result of the tool's use?

6. If you could not picture yourself involved in spiritual warfare before, can you now picture yourself participating in *servant warfare*? If yes, what caused the change in your thinking?

7. Would an "addicted, messed-up person" fit into your congregation? How would members respond to this person?

GO AND CHANGE THE WORLD!

It is the chiefest point of happiness that a man
is willing to be what he is.
— Erasmus —

At Vineyard Community Church in Cincinnati, we have
delivered food to the needy and shut-ins around town for
years. One October afternoon, a call for food came in that seemed
routine until Doug and Ken arrived at the address. Ken shook his
head as he compared the address on the paper to the house number. "It must be correct. Go figure!"

Capturing their full attention was a pink neon sign depicting a
palm reader and advertising the services of *Madame Sheila*. Both
men had heard a lot about the dangers of the occult and were
uncomfortable. Doug's first reaction was, "There is no way we're
giving this food from the church to somebody like that!" But since
they had already made the trip, they reluctantly went in.

Twelve customers were in the waiting room. Sheila's niece, a
single mom, said she had originated the call. Mustering up his
courage, Doug asked why she had called for help. "I heard you
guys helped anyone who needed food," she said. "I'm out of

everything. I didn't know what else to do but call you. It's OK to receive food even if I don't go to your church, isn't it?"

"We give food out to anyone in need, regardless of their faith," Doug answered. "But I can tell you your future looks pretty bleak without Jesus. Before we leave could we pray for you?"

The waiting room clients and Madame Sheila herself watched as Doug and Ken prayed for this young mother in need. Others began requesting prayer, and soon a makeshift prayer circle formed. After some minutes of praying, Doug offered, "Would anyone like to repent and receive Jesus as your Savior?" To his shock, six in the circle nodded their heads yes. He had explained the gospel once, but based on the eagerness of the customers to receive Christ, he figured he must have been unclear in his explanation. After this second presentation of the gospel, eight wanted to receive Christ! So right there in the waiting room of Madame Sheila's place, eight new believers came into God's kingdom.

Christians showing mercy to a palm reader and her customers— a surprising combination? In a dark world where millions of lives are closed off to God, we need to find ways of penetrating hearts with the life of Christ. Two bags of groceries built a bridge into a dark home. I have found that serving in the name of Jesus Christ is a powerful means of doing spiritual warfare. As a result of practical love shown by Christians, walls of spiritual resistance often come down.

A few years ago I would have approached Madame Sheila very differently. I would have skipped bringing the food and come at her with a dozen Bible verses, a few choice gospel tracts, an aggressive attitude, and at least a little fear. There is a place for verses, written materials, and enthusiasm, but they best follow in the wake of Christians tearing down walls of darkness by meeting practical needs.

ME? CHANGE THE WORLD?
YOU'VE GOT TO BE KIDDING!

Let's be honest, when we hear the words *spiritual warfare* we don't usually rush to sign up for battle. More likely we think, "I'm a civilian, not a soldier. Count me out."

But before Jesus ascended to heaven, he issued a battle call to every Christian to "go into all the world and preach the good news to every creature" (Mk 16:15). He called us to invade this spiritually dark and hostile world. He also promised us adequacy for the task. "Signs will follow... they will cast out demons... the sick will get well" (v. 17). Jesus called us to a simply profound task. His call is very direct: "Go and change the world!"

I've met few Christians who feel qualified to conduct spiritual warfare. Most feel like the basset hound described in this article:

As dogs go, basset hounds are built for comfort, not for speed. So it was no doubt with some distress that Tattoo the basset hound found his leash caught in the door of his master's car Wednesday night. The car was moving, at one point about 25 mph. Tacoma police motorcycle officer Kerry Filbert spotted the dog "picking 'em up and putting 'em down" along side the vehicle. When the driver's wife realized what had happened, she cried out, "Tattoo! Tattoo!"

When I told the driver he was dragging his dog, he said, "Now that you mention it, I did hear something banging around back there," Filbert said. The Renton couple had been visiting friends when they absentmindedly let Tattoo out of the car to relieve himself and forgot to put him back in the seat. The dog was relatively unhurt, although he did suffer some tire damage, Filbert said. The officer recommended the dog be checked out at a local animal hospital.[1]

When it comes to spiritual warfare, do you feel like Tattoo, the basset hound? As a one-time basset owner I can assure you that God did not design the basset body to run, period—much less behind a car! A basset's legs are barely long enough to lift its tube-shaped body off the ground. For a few minutes this dog may be able to approximate the performance of a greyhound, but not for long. When trying to follow some of the popular models for spiritual warfare you may have felt like Tattoo, but I don't think that was God's intent.

It doesn't take a rocket scientist to see that Jesus' call to change the world has been largely ignored by the modern church. Most Christians conclude that battling darkness is a discipline fit only for the body of Christ's "elite." We see this as a task for the special forces of the church—God's Green Berets!

◆◆◆

Jesus' call to change the world has been largely ignored by the modern church.

◆◆◆

As a pastor I contributed to this belief in the experts-only approach to spiritual warfare until one Sunday when I saw the error in that mindset. My church was full of twenty-somethings, but we had one older lady who had been a Christian longer than most of us had been alive. That Sunday I finished a sermon series on spiritual warfare, ending with a challenge to become powerful spiritual warriors.

Sue approached me with a no-nonsense look that only a veteran can give. "After years of trying to be a warrior," she said, "I'm just plain tired of it all. I don't have the 'rah, rah' enthusiasm any longer. How about if I just sew curtains for people? Do you think I could make a difference by just serving people?"

My first thought was, "Who ever heard of making a difference by sewing? Maybe it's called 'sewing in the Spirit!'" In spite of my skeptical response, over the next few days the Lord began to speak to me about the unrealistic mentality I had conveyed to my congregation. When I took off my pastor-teacher hat, I could see clearly that I'd been eliminating people from usefulness in God's kingdom by perpetuating several myths about the kind of person God uses. I had been broadcasting a false message: *God uses only the strong, the experts, the courageous, the powerful.*

As we consider stepping out to change the world let's look more closely at the excuses we hide behind.

A JOURNEY ALONG THE YELLOW BRICK ROAD

I'm a *big* movie buff. In fact, I have some old refurbished theater seats in my basement to enhance my movie watching. All my favorite movies are at least thirty years old. Near the top of my list is one of the most-watched movies of all time, *The Wizard of Oz.* I first saw this 1939 classic was when I was in the first grade. I remember begging my parents for days to let me see it. They were cautious because I was prone to nightmares, but my begging prevailed. They were right to be reluctant: I watched most of it peeking through my fingers.

The Wicked Witch of the West, who represents the power of darkness, scared the daylights out of me. As soon as Dorothy began her journey to the Emerald City, the Witch showed up to threaten her with the promise, "Dorothy, you'll never see Kansas or Auntie Em again!" With no other options and overwhelming odds, she took the advice of the Munchkins and followed the yellow brick road.

The characters in this film had one thing in common: They all saw themselves as incomplete. Until each one's missing part was found, they were left out of life. In our Christian life, many of us offer similar excuses for our non-involvement in changing the world.

Dorothy: "I'm not strong enough!" As Dorothy began her journey with Toto in hand, she had an unforgettable look of shock on her face. The harder she tried to find power with self-talk ("I've got to be strong, I've got to be strong"), the more aware she was of her limitations. It wasn't until Dorothy looked beyond herself to the needs of others that she found inner strength that was sufficient for waging war with the witch.

◆◆◆

If you only have a little time left, why not use it
to serve other like there's no tomorrow?

◆◆◆

I have seen many Dorothys stuck in their limitations. For example, my friend Ruby came to know Christ in her late fifties, not long before she was to retire. She joined a charismatic church that talked a lot about defeating darkness and even offered training in spiritual warfare. She was grateful to be retired because she now had plenty of time to study and train for effective Christian service. But as year after year passed, and Ruby added lots of training but next to no actual ministry, she developed a bad case of the "Dorothys." The more she thought about what might lie ahead, the more unprepared she felt. For years Ruby learned about spiritual warfare in great detail, but she was never given a challenge or a specific opportunity to actually put it into action.

When I met her, she was in her seventies and in failing health. She told me with tears in her eyes, "The doctors think I don't have much time left. My heart is failing." I don't know what got into me, but instead of expressing great compassion for her, I felt urged to challenge her.

"Well, if you only have a little time left," I said, "why not use it to serve others like there's no tomorrow? Feed the poor. Pray for the sick. Lead people to Christ. Go out with a bang!"

To my surprise, instead of getting mad Ruby began to do what

I'd suggested. The very next Saturday she went with a team to care for single moms and pray for the sick. One woman Ruby prayed for was in her nineties and hadn't managed to flex her ankle in years. When suddenly the old woman could move her foot, Ruby was overjoyed and convinced that God could use even her. Within weeks, not only was the world changing around her, Ruby's body was changing—for the better.

Ruby is eighty now, and feeling better than she did when she was in her sixties. She is hands-down the most prolific evangelist in our church. She now considers it a slow week if she doesn't lead at least three people to the Lord! And she seems to be most effective with men and women in their twenties.

The Scarecrow: "I'm not smart enough!" At times I've been a Scarecrow in my approach to spiritual warfare. I have moaned, "If I only had a brain… if only I had more spiritual intelligence… then God could *really* use me." I have never been a spiritual whiz. It seems the things others learn quickly, I pick up slowly. I don't know if there are "spiritual learning disabilities," but if they exist, I might have several.

◆◆◆

If there are "spiritual learning
disabilities," I might have several.

◆◆◆

Consider my first encounter with a demonic power. Late one night during my college years, my roommate Jim confided in me about some severe spiritual struggles he'd been going through and asked if I would pray for him. As I asked the Lord to touch these specific areas, Jim began to groan. His expression changed, his eyes took on a glassy appearance, and he seemed unwilling to look at me. Though he had no training in foreign language, Jim was speaking in what sounded like fluent Spanish. I asked him what was going on and he said his name was *Diablo*—Spanish for *devil.*

For years I had read about Jesus and the apostles encountering and defeating demons. I had even secretly wished that one day God would use me to do similar acts of power. Now that the time was upon me, I felt like the dog who had barked and chased the neighbor's car for years until one day the neighbor let him catch up: "Well, now that I've caught it, what do I do with it?"

I called my friend Rick from our campus Bible study, who I'd heard had experience dealing with demons. When he arrived at my room he looked less than enthusiastic. "You *have* done this before, haven't you?" I asked.

"Well, sort of. Actually, I've just watched someone else pray in a situation like this."

"That's close enough for me," I assured him. At midnight you go with what's available! For the next three hours, we paused periodically to ask each other what we should do next as we stumbled forward identifying the specific demonic powers and commanding them to leave. Finally, at 3:00 A.M., Jim seemed to be freed of whatever it was that had gripped him.

In the days following our prayer session, I couldn't help but feel confused and intimidated by my spiritual battle. Rick recommended I pick up a book or two on spiritual warfare. I discovered there are literally hundreds of books on the subject, and the ones I read made me even more frustrated. I couldn't imagine ever having sufficient spiritual knowledge to deal with the powers of darkness the way these authors prescribed.

Today I realize that being effective in spiritual warfare isn't dependent on spiritual "intelligence." God changes the world through our availability, not our academic knowledge. The Apostle Paul concurs as he writes to fellow believers. "Not many of you were wise by human standards.... But God chose the foolish things of the world to shame the wise; God chose the weak things of the world to shame the strong" (1 Cor 1:26).

For example, one Saturday I led a team of windshield washers on an outreach to a local shopping center. We serve customers for free while they shop, then leave a small card explaining that we cleaned their windshield to show them God's love in a practical way.

Bev was a rookie to serving the community like this, and she was a bit apprehensive. She was especially worried about setting off car alarms. I suggested she stay away from the expensive cars that often have alarms, adding that I'd set off a few myself but no one had ever gotten upset with me.

As you might guess, it wasn't long before Bev set off an alarm. "What do I do now?" she yelled to me across the parking lot. Before I could answer the car's owner came out of the electronics store where we were serving. When he asked what she was doing, all Bev could offer was a stream-of-consciousness answer: "I was just showing God's love—it's for free—there's my pastor over there—the Vineyard church—we're not taking any donations for this."

The man actually seemed to make sense out of her answer and walked back into the store. It turned out he was a salesman in the store along with Bill, a regular at our church. The first thing he asked Bill when he returned was, "Isn't the Vineyard the church you go to?" This guy was the resident skeptic and fond of criticizing any oddity about Christians he read or heard about. Bill had taken it on the chin a few times with him before so he answered, "That depends, why do you ask?"

"Well, some folks from there just washed my windshield to show me God's love in a practical way. All I can say is, I'm impressed." At that Bill said, "Yeah, I go to that church!"

From that from that day on, Bill says, the salesman began to change. "It was as though when his windshield was washed, something happened in his mind and attitude."

The Tinman: "I'm not sensitive enough." The Tinman said, "I need a heart." At times we say in a similar way, "I'm not spiritually sensitive enough to be used by God."

The Tinman was looking for an encounter that would change him permanently. Unless Oz gave him a heart, he felt he would never be complete. Similarly, in our search for world-changing effectiveness we ask God to empower us with spiritual sensitivity in mega-doses. As reasonable as that sounds, I have found that when we seek to be more spiritually perceptive, we often end up being just plain weird.

Shortly after my frustrating first encounter with darkness, a friend told me about a "really powerful spiritual warrior" who owned a bakery in town. To many of my friends, most of whom were new Christians, this man was quite a phenomenon. When I met him, he wasn't a bit bashful about recounting stories of casting demons out of people. He claimed to have a sensitivity that made him far more effective than average Christians. "In fact," he boasted, "I don't even use measuring cups and spoons to bake anymore. I don't look at the gauges on the oven. I don't set timers. I let the Holy Spirit guide me in all I do, including my baking." Not surprisingly, it wasn't long before his bakery went belly-up. I guess "baking in the Spirit" is not one of the gifts of the Lord!

It's easy to think that those who are truly effective in the spiritual realm are a cut above the rest of us. They see and hear things we've never seen. They tell us of their "promptings," and we can't remember a single prompting other than an occasional hunger pang! While God wants us to value and believe in the mystical, I suspect we undervalue the rational and practical. When we do, we add unreasonable conditions to our usefulness to God.

Our view of our effectiveness seems to run counter to Jesus' utterly simple approach. When he sent out the Seventy, he offered them simple instructions: "When you enter a town... tell them,

'The kingdom of God is near you'" (Lk 10:8, 9). He mentions nothing about special gifting here; his technique couldn't have been simpler. The training session must have taken all of a few minutes! Best of all, it worked wonderfully. Jesus' summary was clear: "I saw Satan falling!"

The Lion: "I'm not brave enough." The lion was convinced that if only he had more courage, then everything would go smoothly. His mantra was, "I'm not afraid of spooks. I'm not afraid of spooks. I'm not, I'm not, I'm not, I'm not." But the more he repeated this affirmation, the more fearful he became.

In the wake of my experience with my roommate, I thought I needed greater spiritual courage in order to be effective in Christ's kingdom. Many of the books on spiritual warfare I read said that boldness was crucial. I thought that if I just became spiritually brave I would be able to pummel the powers of darkness.

◆◆◆

The harder we try to become something
we're not, the more discouraged we become.

◆◆◆

Too many of us think that we need to become spiritual super-heroes who single-handedly assault the powers of darkness. While spiritual courage is important, let's not overemphasize it. The harder wc try to become something we're not, the more discouraged we become. I think God calls us to availability, not fearlessness. We can have fear in our hearts and still be effective if we are simply willing to be used by God. Courage, by definition, implies that we do have some fear, but we go forward in spite of it.

My friend Janet is a timid but willing spiritual warrior. What she lacks in bravery she makes up for with great commitment. When I heard she was taking a training course on evangelism I was not surprised when she threw herself into a serious training regimen. For several months she followed a prescribed lengthy prayer time each day, memorized dozens of verses, and practiced evangelistic conversations with her classmates.

After training she began to go door-to-door in the community. One night her partner didn't show up to knock on doors with her, but she reasoned, "I'm prayed up, read up, and faithed up. I'll go by myself!"

The door was open at the first house she approached, so she knocked. She could see through the screen that someone was in a darkened corner of the room so she called out, "Could I take a few minutes of your time and share with you the good news of Jesus Christ?" She heard a mutter back, so with some trepidation she launched into her gospel presentation. When she finished she timidly asked the leading question, "Would you like to respond to this opportunity to receive Christ by praying with me?"

◆◆◆

Courage, by definition, implies that we do
have some fear, but we go forward in spite of it.

◆◆◆

As her eyes adjusted to the darkness she noticed something she had overlooked: This "person" was no person at all, but a parrot perched in the corner! In spite of the fact that the parrot didn't receive Christ, Janet did learn a valuable lesson: God would give her courage to go forward in spite of her apprehension.

BE AVAILABLE, NOT HEROIC

Jesus didn't call us to be the most *heroic* people on the planet, just the most *available*. But often we set conditions before we allow God's love to flow through us to others. The following misconceptions can hinder us.

Misconception #1: "I must be pumped up!" Many of us say we aren't ready to do spiritual warfare because we must be super strong, able to leap tall buildings with a single rebuke! We read verses like "we battle not with flesh and blood, but against spirits and principalities," and assume the only way to take on any of those forces is by sheer might and great spiritual muscle.

This misconception was clearly conveyed to me in the first in-depth teaching I received on spiritual warfare. A friend had recommended a sixteen-tape series by a woman who was an "expert" on the topic. This lady often referred to how much she had learned "in the school of the Lord" about the spiritual realms. She frequently referred to her lengthy fasting sessions and her daily hours of "pressing into the Lord" in prayer. Although her stories were fascinating, the more I listened, the more I became convinced I couldn't do what she did. I became discouraged and eventually concluded that spiritual warfare wasn't my gift.

Misconception #2: "I must be a veteran." The woman on the tapes was beyond the expert level of experience; she was a virtual guru of the faith. She said, "It takes years to learn to effectively battle the powers of darkness!" Her expertise made my early attempts seem feeble and amateurish.

Misconception #3: "I must have remarkable endurance." Many of the woman's stories entailed marathon sessions in prayer. I like to pray, but even as a pastor I find it difficult to pray for more than thirty minutes at a time. As a sufferer of Attention Deficit Disorder, I can't use any model of ministry that requires lengthy bouts of concentration. Unfortunately, in the church and in the media, lengthy battles with the powers of darkness have been held up as models.

Endurance is what millions of Americans saw when ABC's Tom Jarriel hosted a *20/20* episode that focused on a teenage girl who had demonic problems. The one-hour segment focused on a girl named "Gina" who was afflicted with demonic powers.[2] She spoke in various languages, in various voices, and at times demonstrated incredible strength.

The praying went on for hours. I grew weary just watching the struggle! In time, as the people surrounding Gina prayed for her, the demonic presence seemed to leave her. In an interview at the end of the show she reported she felt free and once again in her right mind. These folks didn't seem to mind the marathon prayer sessions. "We've been doing this for years," they said. "It's kind of what we do."

◆◆◆

He empowers us as we look beyond
ourselves to the needs of others.

◆◆◆

While that may be true for those prayer warriors, most of us who love Jesus find it hard to relate. The good news is, God doesn't ask us to have amazing endurance or to be "pumped up" or to be particularly strong. Rather, he blesses us when we are willing to serve and empowers us as we look beyond ourselves to the needs of others.

Now that we've looked at some common excuses for avoiding spiritual warfare, let's take a look at spiritual warfare itself.

CAN WE AVOID SPIRITUAL WARFARE?

As Jesus gazed at the apostles in his last moments with them, he understood he was imparting the future of his kingdom to a crop of available men who were far short of expert status in anything but fishing. The spirit behind Jesus' instructions (see Matthew 28:18-20) on how to reach the world was simple: "Go and do a small thing. As you touch the people along your path, I will orchestrate my work in your midst and cause your many small things to add up to a great thing that only God could build. I will change the world through you, one life at a time."

Research done by Peter Wagner indicates that only about 10 percent of Christians see themselves as effective evangelists. If such a small number within the ranks of believers see themselves as naturals at sharing Christ, imagine what percentage feel at home doing what seems to be even more intimidating—spiritual warfare? But God has planned to enlist 100 percent of Christians in spiritual warfare so we can penetrate the darkness around us. In spite of any fears we have, being involved in spiritual warfare is unavoidable.

We *already live* in a spiritual world. The world is teeming with the activity of angels, both good and evil. The Book of Revelation is clear that Satan and his forces will one day be put into captivity for eternity, but not until the end of time (see Revelation 20:7-10). All people, Christian or not, are ultimately spiritual beings and have a natural hunger for God and an attraction to seek spiritual things (see 1 Thessalonians 5:18).

We are *already involved* in a spiritual conflict. From the moment Adam and Eve rebelled against God in the Garden and God promised that he would "crush" the serpent, a great cosmic war has been going on around us. It is a spiritual civil war that pits darkness against light, the forces of holiness against the Evil One and his hordes. The battleground of this conflict is the souls of humankind.

There is no neutral ground in this war. The moment you said "yes" to Jesus you said "yes" to being in this battle. The Evil One considers you his enemy, and his forces resist you and what you stand for as a follower of Jesus Christ. Maybe you would not have voted yourself into the fray, but reluctance doesn't change anything.

Scott Alexander, author of *Rhinoceros Success,*[3] says there are two kinds of people on earth: *rhinos* and *cows.* Rhinos accept the reality that life is a jungle. Rhinos aren't in love with the idea of war, but they are willing to charge into the jungle of life. Cows, on the other hand, live in denial over the true state of things. "Warfare?" they say. "I don't see any war going on around me." Cows, like the majority of us, seek a safe approach to life. They take few, if any, risks. However, cows are every bit as vulnerable to the harsh realities of life, because the lions who dwell in the jungle always know where to find fresh food: in the cow pasture.

We are *already filled* with the Holy Spirit. God has filled us with his Spirit in order to be effective rhinos for his kingdom in the world. He has declared full-fledged war on the powers of darkness. Jesus said, "I have come to destroy the works of darkness." In Mark 16 Jesus gives notice that from then on the conflict is not the responsibility of one man, but of a race of new people, Christians, who will take on the enemy of the human soul. On his last night with the apostles Jesus asked the Father to send the Holy Spirit to be with us forever (see John 15:15-17). He has given us the weapons of warfare we need to invade the darkness around us.

Recently we were doing servant warfare in our community by washing cars for free and offering to pray for those we served. Like many we encounter, Bob was taken aback when we refused to take money for our services and told him we did this to show God's love in a practical way. In the conversation that followed, we were able to share the gospel with this man and lead him in prayer on the spot to receive Christ.

As we were praying with him, Bob began to make growling sounds, and it became obvious that demonic powers were present. We took him inside our nearby building for further prayer. As we conversed, Bob confided that he'd suffered irrational fears and obsessive thought patterns for years. After about an hour, Bob emerged with a born-again heart and freedom from his crippling fears.

I would like to have been a mouse in the corner when Bob got home.

"Honey, what took you so long?"

"Well, I was on my way to the hardware store when I stopped for a free car wash some Christians put on to show God's love in a practical way. I ended up giving my life to Christ, and then I had a couple of demons cast out of me. Other than that, it's been a pretty standard Saturday so far."

Bob and his wife Carol joined our church the following weekend. They brought their extended family with them and were actively involved for several years before moving out of the area.

◆◆◆

I ended up giving my life to Christ, and then I had a couple of demons cast out of me. Other than that, it's been a pretty standard Saturday so far.

◆◆◆

A free car wash is a small thing. That small thing opened the door to another small thing: praying for Bob. That prayer led him to open his heart to Christ and to be set free from demonic powers.

DON'T STARE AT THE HEADLIGHTS!

Most of us aren't against the idea of being a force for God in the world; we just don't know how to get started. The church seems to be stuck in what my grandma calls a *sitchiation*. She is from a north Texas town where colorful colloquialisms abound.

"A sitchiation," she explains, "is a *situation* that's gotten out of control. It's when you know you need to do something to get out of a jam, but you don't have the foggiest idea how to go about making a change."

Last New Year's Eve I was driving home after a late-night service. As I came over a hill, a huge whitetail was in my lane. Considering the dangerous position the buck had taken up, I wondered if he'd been to a New Year's Eve party that evening! His response to my approach was typical of deer that look into headlights: He froze. If he could talk I suspect he would have said, "I always forget what to do next when I see headlights." That deer was stuck in a *sitchiation*.

In the Christian life we are prone to numerous headlight staredowns. We look at lists of "requirements" for being a useful soldier in God's army and we are left paralyzed. But if we remember that Jesus' assignment is to do a small thing, we are liberated from our *sitchiations* to step out and make a difference. We need to set aside our understandings of spiritual warfare that overwhelm and impair us and take on the more productive role of *servant warriors*.

An effective servant warfare project we do at Vineyard takes place every Wednesday at noon when a group of us who work in downtown Cincinnati take part of our lunch breaks to feed parking meters. Each volunteer receives a couple of rolls of dimes and a stack of business cards that say, "Your parking meter looked hungry, so we fed it!" On the back of the card is a brief explanation, a map to our location, worship service times, and a phone number.

One of my parking meter team members is Scott, a bright young litigator who works for one of the largest law firms in Cincinnati. Every Wednesday Scott leaves the world of attorneys, courtrooms, and corporate clients to serve others in small ways. God is using his simple availability to change the world.

A couple of days after a recent parking meter outing with Scott, a note came in the mail from a lady whose life was touched by our simple service. "Today is my birthday," she wrote. "For the first time in my life everybody forgot my birthday. My husband forgot, my children forgot, even my parents forgot… but God didn't forget me. I'm not a very religious person, but today God got my attention in a big way when you fed my meter. Thank you."

Small things done with great love build bridges into darkened lives. It could be taking food to a palm reader, washing a car, or feeding a parking meter. *When we step out to do a small thing, God shows up to accomplish a big thing.*

Pair and Share Questions

1. What is your first response to the words *spiritual warfare*?

2. Have you had any experiences dealing with spiritual darkness? What happened? What did you learn?

3. Do you agree with the statement, "Jesus has called each of us to change the world"? Why or why not?

4. Have you ever felt that Jesus has called you to change the world? Explain.

5. If you've used excuses about why you couldn't participate in the spiritual battle, with whom would you most align yourself?

   • *Dorothy,* who needed strength

   • *Scarecrow,* who lacked intelligence

   • *Tinman,* who was short on sensitivity

   • *Lion,* who didn't have enough courage

6. Explain what you understand to be the difference between spiritual warfare and servant warfare.

7. Plan a "small thing done with great love" with your group.

Carry out the plan and share your experiences. (Appendix One contains several possible projects.)

8. Recount a small thing someone did for you that made a difference in your life. How did it affect you?

CHASING THE RIGHT GAME

You've got to be very careful if you don't know where
you are going, because you might not get there.

— Yogi Berra —

*"I don't think you can do that here! I'd better check with the
boss."*

The group Ken leads decided to adjourn to Bob's Big Boy
restaurant for dessert one evening. As they ate and talked and
laughed, they couldn't help but notice the harried look on their
waitress' face.

"Are you OK?" someone asked as she whizzed by.

"I'm OK, it's just that our dishwasher quit tonight in the
middle of his shift and all the servers are now serving *and* washing.
It's a little overwhelming, but it'll be all right."

That was all the information Ken's group needed. As soon as
they finished their pie and paid the bill they sprang into action.
Two guys took on the dishwasher, several young women toted
plastic dish containers from table to table, and before long the
dirty dish situation was under control.

The waitress walked past the head volunteer dishwasher in the
kitchen and with a startled look on her face asked, "Aren't you the

guy at table ten? Why are you back here, doing dishes?"

"Because you needed some help! We believe God's love is better shown than just talked about. Besides, didn't you say the dishwasher quit tonight?"

"Well, yes, but I don't think we can let you just do the dishes like this. I'd better go check with the boss."

Within a few minutes that waitress had begun gossiping the gospel to all the other servers. "They're doing it to show us God's love in a practical way!"

A few minutes later the boss and a growing number of servers came to watch the small group in action. "Tell me one more time, *why* are you doing this?" the manager asked. He pulled out a three-ring restaurant policy notebook. As he thumbed through it he said again, "I don't know if you can do this for free like this."

"Well, by the time you find out, we'll be done."

As the group left the restaurant, it was obvious that everyone, including the customers, had heard about the exploits of the dishwashing team from table ten. Heads turned, strangers smiled, and many waved goodbye.

◆◆◆

*We believe God's love is better shown
than just talked about.*

◆◆◆

As Ken related this story to me, he glowed. "The atmosphere in that place was electric. You could feel the presence of God, right there in Bob's Big Boy!"

"What you saw at the restaurant," I said, "was real spiritual warfare taking place through your dishwashing."

"No kidding! As we've gone back since that night, I've noticed the servers always stop by our table to chat. Now that I think about it, they usually ask us a question or two about God."

Although most of the people in that small group are new Christians, they've already discovered a truth about spiritual warfare: *The power of kindness can remove spiritual barriers that prevent people from seeing God clearly.* Taking away people's spiritual blinders will ultimately help them receive Christ.

By serving in kindness we're building bridges to the unchurched that will transport them toward a relationship with God. Some have blinders that prevent them from even seeing they need a bridge. Like the Apostle Paul, they need the scales to fall from their eyes (see Acts 9:17-19).

Just before returning to heaven, Jesus gave the church a challenge and an invitation. Essentially it was this: "*I* will change the world as *you* are available to express my life in the world by doing small things in my name!"

Jesus used many metaphors to express his simple plan for changing the world. Like the farmer, as *we* plant and water the seeds of God's life, *he* brings about a human harvest. Like the fisherman, as *we* throw out our nets, *he* causes men and women to come into the net of God's life.

God has called us to make a difference, but as we step out to obey him we run into the confusion of a second *sitchiation* in spiritual warfare. We say, *"I'd like to change the world, but I don't know how."*

BOBO SJOGREN, THE HUNTING-IMPAIRED DOG

I grew up in Kansas in a family that often the state's most popular big game: pheasants. You may not consider pheasants big game, but keep in mind this was Kansas! They are the closest thing to big game in the wheat state.

One year my dad and I decided to buy a hunting dog especially bred for pointing out pheasants. After some research, we found that a Brittany Spaniel was probably the best breed for what we had in mind. With anticipation we picked out a pedigreed pup and set out to train a world-class hunting dog. We sent Bobo off to dog training school and he returned home with a good report card. According to the trainers, he showed excellent potential as a pheasant dog.

On his first hunt, however, something went wrong. Bobo chased down a wounded rabbit. Eventually he returned from that rabbit trail, but he had the taste of rabbit blood in his mouth. Bobo was never the same. Every pheasant hunt became a frustrating chase after rabbits! Rabbits are fine, but we were pheasant hunters. Bobo became scent-impaired, and was useless as a pheasant dog. He could still chase pheasants, but he was addicted to rabbits. At the first scent of one he was off and running for miles, chasing what was usually uncatchable.

Bobo could have benefited from the pet counseling services some psychologists in Los Angeles are now offering. (Where else *but* in Los Angeles!) He was a good dog; he was just confused. I suspect if we'd sent Bobo in for counseling, the dog psychologist would have challenged him to think through three areas of confusion:

What is your goal?
What is the best path to get there?
What is the right strategy?

As Christians we have been called to change the world, but we suffer with a similar scent impairment. We forget what we're here to do, we overlook our assignment, and we seem to be constantly chasing rabbits!

◆◆◆

*We are out to change the way
people think about God.*

◆◆◆

Bobo needed to clarify the game he was after: *pheasants.* We too need to clarify what we are aiming for in servant warfare: *people.* In particular we are out to change the way people think about God. As Ken's small group washed dishes they were changing the way the employees and customers of that restaurant thought about

God. They were wielding the weapon of God's kindness. Remember, servant warfare is *using the power of kindness to penetrate the spiritually darkened hearts of people with the love of God.*

Let's pull apart that sentence and look at the implications behind the pregnant definition.

DEFINING THE GOAL

"... to penetrate the spiritually darkened hearts of people...."

Unless we constantly remember to value people, we are destined to go off track. It's easy to forget that people are the central focus. It seems that without periodic reminders, Christians are prone to misuse the power of God.

For example, a few months ago after a service, a woman stuck out her hand and said, "Hi, my name is Jill. This is my husband Erik. He *isn't* a believer." I thought it was odd that she said something so harsh in front of her husband. She went on to describe in detail her "deep" mystical Christian life. Later Erik confided, "My wife gives me heck and talks about me like I'm unspiritual, but you should meet her when she has PMS!" In a rush to acquire gifts and supposed maturity, Jill had missed the most central lesson of all: What matters most to God are *people*, including her husband.

The Bible makes it clear that people are what it's all about. In spiritual warfare our focus is on people, period. If we don't put supreme value on people, we are destined for confusion and we will never change the world. Granted, in a world full of broken, irritating people it's easy to forget that this truth is central in God's heart.

President Clinton attributed his successful presidential campaign to a simple slogan on the wall of his headquarters in Little Rock: "It's the economy, stupid!" Christians would benefit from a similar poster: "It's people, *period!*"

We are to *penetrate* human hearts. Often the attitudes and

actions of a servant reach into the hearts of people more quickly than a well-developed argument or even a power-packed prayer. It's one thing to speak words, but it's quite another to make a lasting impression.

Recently some hearts were penetrated as we cleaned toilets at Bob's Blues Bar. When I approached the bartender at Silky's with my unique offer, it was obvious I had pierced her heart. She scrutinized my cleaning supplies, then glanced back at me again. I could see the wheels turning in her head. Several people sitting nearby leaned over to eavesdrop. After a moment of silence she asked, "Do you need a drink or something?" She went on, "Let me get this straight. You are Christians who want to clean our toilets? I don't get it. I thought church people were against drinking, smoking, and the things that go on in bars."

"Actually, we don't necessarily advocate going to bars, but we love people who go to bars. We especially love people who work in bars!"

◆◆◆

It's one thing to speak words, but it's quite
another to make a lasting impression.

◆◆◆

I call her reaction a *tilt*—that is, the response from unbelievers when we encounter them in a kindness project. Sometimes the tilt is a puzzled look. Other times it's a laugh, a mouth dropping open, or even eyes tearing up. Whatever the response, a tilt is evidence that God is rewiring spiritual perspectives. Serving creates a tilt. A tilt starts the process of redefining who God is in a darkened heart.

Most unbelievers think that Christians generally stand for two things: #1, telling others how to live, and #2, fund raising. When we serve unbelievers without coming across as scolding parents, or begging for money, we might just engage their hearts and make a lasting impression.

CHOOSING THE BEST PATH

If the goal of spiritual warfare is to *change people*, then the most efficient way to get there is *"… using the power of kindness.…"*

One hot July day, Thom, a new Christian, decided to redeem a couple of hours of free time and give away soft drinks at a local park. He stopped by our building to pick up ice chests, cans of soda, and cards that explained the drink giveaway. By himself, this shy man took off to bring the love of God to thirsty Cincinnatians.

The local CBS affiliate's reporters were doing a story on people's responses to the sweltering summer heat when they came across Thom dragging his plastic cooler around the lake. "Why are you doing this?" they asked.

"I have a feeling that if Jesus were here today he'd be passing out cool drinks. I like to give God's love away in practical ways. Besides, it's a lot of fun!"

The video clip ended with Thom's words. The newscasters were so taken by the image, words, and sentiment that when the live studio feed came on, the newscasters were silent for a couple of moments. Looking stunned, one said, "Well, that's a creative way to deal with the summer heat, now, isn't it!"

◆◆◆

*"If Jesus were here today he'd
be passing out cool drinks."*

◆◆◆

There is great power in being kind. People whose hearts are closed often become open and vulnerable when they are shown simple kindness.

There's no denying that darkness is real; however, given the choice we would all rather run away from it if we had the opportunity. During the twentieth century, our culture has been far out on a rational limb. We have come to believe that if we can't measure it with our five senses, it isn't real. The more scientifically centered we become, the more our souls hunger for hope. Intuitively every human knows there is more to reality than meets the eye. The more we hear the spirit world doesn't exist, the more curious we become about what we hear *isn't* out there. For the past several years, books on the spirit world have been selling like hot cakes. Millions of copies of New Age books such as *The Celestine Prophecy* and *Embraced by the Light* have sold in recent years to spiritually hungry seekers who desire hope for life beyond the here and now.

Officially American culture doesn't put much stock in the supernatural; off the record, we are nearly obsessed with it! Time-Life Books, famous for their various mail order book series, reports that books on the occult and the nether world are big sellers year after year. We all know from childhood experiences, the harder we try not to think about flying pink elephants, the more we are absorbed with them.

Sometimes even Christians become engrossed with speculation about darkness. Over the past several years a number of Christian novels on spiritual warfare have been big sellers. In general, I have no problem with Christians reading novels on spiritual warfare. But when we only gather information about the spirit world and never do much about it at a practical level, we become anxious. My friend Mary became absorbed with one of these novels. Though she was a veteran Christian, she had never had any direct dealings with the powers of darkness. She put down her copy of the novel and hopped in her car while thinking about the powers of darkness. As she pulled out of her garage, a dark form leapt across the windshield. As Mary screeched on her brakes, she rebuked the devil. She was a little chagrined to find the demon was only her cat Fluffy!

As a pastor I constantly hear Christians attempt to take the normal events of life and make them seem like a spiritual attack. A few months ago, coincidentally, two of my three children broke their arms within three days of each other—one playing soccer, the other jumping out of a swing. I wasn't surprised to hear several members of my congregation offer their spiritual insight by suggesting I was under attack. My response to them was, "No, not spiritual warfare—just soccer! Life happens!" We have difficulty distinguishing between spiritual warfare and the normal effects of living in a fallen world.

◆◆◆

The harder we try not to think about flying,
pink elephants, the more we are
absorbed with them.

◆◆◆

Spiritual darkness is often talked about in Christian circles, but the understanding of what that means varies greatly. For years I debated with friends about terminology differences between someone being *possessed* versus *oppressed.* We agreed that a Christian can be oppressed by Satan (afflicted), but never possessed by Satan (controlled). That terminology is not in keeping with the original language of the Greek New Testament. One word in the Greek New Testament to describe the activities of the world of darkness is *daimonizesthal.* An English rendering of that word could be "demonized." This word describes a broad spectrum of demonic influences meaning *any false view about God that has been brought on by the harsh activity of demons.* Darkness, at its root, is a false image about God that has been perpetuated long enough that eventually that internal image creates an outward pattern of living. From a spiritual perspective those who don't yet know Christ are in need of spiritual liberation to free them from their bondage.

Freedom comes in a variety of ways. Some people, like a prominent businessman in our city, come to freedom uneventfully. He openly told me, "I've been attending your church for awhile, but I am not personally a Christian." Naturally curious, I asked him why he was attending the Vineyard if he was so adamant about not believing in Jesus. "I've been through a rugged divorce recently.

For some reason when I come to church I feel a great deal of peace, even though I don't agree with some of what you say." Several years after our initial conversation that man finally gave his life to Christ during one of our weekend celebrations. He recently pulled me aside and thanked me for hanging in there with him in the past and confided that his recent faith in Jesus has made all the difference in the world. Of course, my question was, "What happened to change your mind about God?" He said, "All I can say is I spent enough time in the environment of love and mercy at the Vineyard that finally the light came on for me."

◆◆◆

*As followers of Jesus we are called to liberate
all who are under the power of darkness
with the life of Christ in us.*

◆◆◆

Sometimes freedom comes dramatically as in the case of Sue, the wife of a well-known rock guitarist. She came forward one Friday after a service to request prayer. After hearing her story I suspected she might have demonic problems, so I called upon the Lord with a simple prayer: "Lord, come by your power and let any darkness be manifest now." When there is no measurable amount of darkness present, there is no reaction to that prayer. But in this case my prayer brought a quick and bizarre response.

Sue began to hiss and slither about on the floor like a snake. I heard, "You can't have her—she's mine!" I thought, "This is just great. The Lord has answered my prayer, but what do I do now?" Inside I was panicking as everyone present was watching me with the "you're the expert—do something!" look. Though I didn't know what to do next, I kept my cool and grabbed a couple of ladies on the prayer team and we moved the woman to a back room where we wouldn't disturb others. For the next several hours we prayed every prayer we knew to pray. We went off in every imaginable direction. We bound the power of this and that. We quoted Bible verses galore. Nothing seemed to have any effect on this tortured woman. My first prayer that evening was "Stir it up, Lord." My closing prayer that night was, "Never mind the first prayer, Lord. Now bring your peace!" To my surprise, as quickly as the odd behavior started, it stopped. As I returned home that evening I felt embarrassed. God had answered my prayer by allowing darkness to be manifest, *but I didn't know how to intelligently deal with it.*

Some days later when we reconvened with Sue, I was amazed to see her looking calm and normal. What a contrast from our Friday night prayer session. This time we changed tactics. We asked, "Has this behavior gone on long? Did something happen in your life that brought this on? Are you willing to change?" In probing into her experience we discovered that although she talked like a spiritual person and seemed to fit the part of a Christian, Sue had *never received Christ.* After leading her in a simple prayer of salvation we prayed for freedom to come to her, and she was quickly liberated of her darkness.

I had started out seeking to cast out a demon. But in the end it was a simple, small thing that made the difference for Sue. She prayed a simple prayer, Jesus came into her heart, and she was changed.

Spiritual warfare isn't necessarily about casting demons out of the Sues of life, nor is it about learning special prayers that guarantee successful encounters with dark powers. It is mostly about doing small things with great love and opening darkened lives to the life of God. As followers of Jesus, we are called to liberate all who are under the power of darkness with the life of Christ in us.

"... with the love of God."

Darkened hearts change when they come in contact with the love of God. That love can take many forms, but ultimately it is only God's love that changes lives. Unless we link spiritual warfare to the love of God, we are using the Holy Spirit's power for something less than what God had in mind when he released the dynamic of the Holy Spirit upon the church (see Mark 16).

As a boy growing up, I was amazed at anything that went *boom!* My friends and I looked forward to the Fourth of July, not because we were patriotic, but because we just loved firecrackers. One year I hit the jackpot when someone gave me a box of M80s he had brought back from a trip to Mexico. An M80 is far more than a firecracker; it is actually a fraction of a stick of dynamite. It was originally intended as a tool to help farmers remove stubborn tree stumps. Of course, my friends and I found all sorts of creative uses for M80s that were illegal and downright dangerous. One M80 in a mailbox and BAM!—no mailbox. We were misusing the power of the M80.

When we practice spiritual warfare but forget that its intent is to bring people to Christ, we misuse the weapons provided to us. God's power has been entrusted to us as the tool to free people from darkness, that they might see their need for salvation in Christ.

The modern church might give us several different answers to the question, "What's the secret to success?" But Jesus' final words make clear that there is only one word that accurately defines the goal of spiritual warfare: *conversion.* God's intent is for us to win darkened souls, not battles. Since humankind fell in Eden, God has sought to make a way for every human being to know him.

A veteran pastor from England named Eddie told me about an old friend of his whose life demonstrates the effectiveness of staying on this simple track. Eddie and three of his friends came to Christ several decades ago. All four men aspired to serve God by pursuing a pastoral ministry, so all applied and were accepted by theological schools in their native England.

To earn money before school, Tom took on a job at a brewery as a janitor. During the summer, he found himself cleaning more than the floors. Tom loved the hardened factory workers in a variety of practical ways. He launched a lawn bowling league that many men in the plant joined. He spent time with them before and after practices, and he showed them he really cared. By the end of the summer Tom had led a dozen of his co-workers to Christ.

Tom began to ask himself, "Why leave this fruitful setting to pursue an official pastoral ministry? This is a big open door from the Lord." So Tom announced to his friends that he was putting off seminary for a semester in order to take care of the new believers in his life. As Christmas rolled around, his friends came home full of enthusiasm about their seminary training. Tom said, "I'll meet up with you guys in the fall semester. I still feel called to minister at the brewery." The fall came and went, as did the next year, and the next. The years became decades and still Tom was faithful to his post at the brewery.

Finally, in his early fifties, Tom retired from the beer factory and fulfilled his dream of going to seminary. Upon ordination in the Church of England, a vicar is required to show evidence of fruitfulness. Most young pastors bring along a person or two they were nice to over the years, but not Tom. With little prompting, several busloads of men and women from the brewery filled the church the day Tom was ordained. Person after person approached the microphone and told of finding Christ through Tom. The ordaining officials had never heard of such fruitfulness.

Tom is an incredible example of someone who practices servant warfare. In the harsh environment of a beer factory, he was able to quietly serve his way into the tough hearts of dozens of the working-class. His strategy for winning them was to penetrate the darkness in their lives by loving them in practical ways. Tom consistently showed these men the love of God until barriers came down and the light of God's kingdom shined into their hearts.[1]

USING THE RIGHT STRATEGY

Not only was my hunting dog unclear about his goal—pheasants—but he was clueless about how to best point them out.

Brittany Spaniels tend to be high-strung. Sometimes Bobo would get so excited about hunting he would begin to run in circles. At that point he couldn't remember his name, much less how to hunt effectively.

As someone who had always aspired to make a difference in life, the news that I could change the world through the power of Christ made me as excited as Bobo before a hunt. My evolution took me from being *meek* to *manic* to *macho* to *mellow*.

The Meek: *"Darkness? I don't see any darkness."* I began the Christian life hoping there were no "things that go bump in the night," but it didn't take much Bible reading to discover that the spirit world is a reality. When I met Christ over twenty years ago, most Christians I knew took the meek approach to spiritual darkness: They simply didn't talk about it. The prevailing strategy was simple: "Ignore it. What we can't see won't hurt us." But darkness is real and it's here to stay.

◆◆◆

There are exactly as many demonic entities
on earth today as there were in Jesus' time.

◆◆◆

In a perfect world there would be no demonic forces to deal with. After all, there is already ample human brokenness on earth without another force to reckon with. Despite our wishes and fears, however, there are exactly as many demonic entities on earth today as there were in Jesus' time. When demons are cast out, they aren't annihilated or locked up in a spiritual jail. They simply leave one location for another, as in the case of the Gadarene demoniac. When Jesus cast out this man's demons, they filled a herd of nearby pigs (see Mark 5:11-13). One day all demons will be locked up in the pit (see Revelation 20:10) but until then, they are loose to do their evil work. The demonic is all around us, and the meek person is understandably fearful.

The Manic: *"Darkness is everywhere!"* A friend of mine says, "I'm not paranoid; it's just that I don't like all those eyes watching me constantly." Once I got in touch with the fact that demons do exist and they are actively doing evil, I was overwhelmed.

Some Christians overreact to darkness. They see every flat tire and broken toaster as the result of demonic activity. This kind of paranoia paralyzed me for awhile. My motto became, "I can't handle this. Let's just hide from darkness." But there is no hiding. Hiding only produces an us-versus-them mentality and keeps us from having a meaningful impact in the world. We see ourselves as the few faithful followers of Jesus in a big, bad world we prefer to stay away from.

◆◆◆

Some Christians... see every flat tire and broken toaster as the result of demonic activity.

◆◆◆

The manic response to darkness causes us to fall prey to "Hail Mary" strategies. When the clock is ticking away in the final quarter of a football game and the home team is trailing, it's time for an act of desperation. Hoping to pull off a miracle, the quarterback heaves a long pass into a crowd of receivers and defensive players.

This mentality is typical of those who live in the manic mindset. In the past couple of years I have heard of three plans to evangelize the entire US before the end of the century. One group I read about planned to reach the country in a single weekend! I admire their enthusiasm, but the "we-need-a-miracle" approach is often a sign of poor strategic thinking.

The Macho: *"Darkness is hard of hearing."* Once I saw that the powers of darkness could be altered by my prayers, I became a little loud, a little pushy. Confidence is great, but I was nearly arrogant. My strategy became, "Search for darkness and *attack* it!" I had taken a good discovery and gone too far. I thought that the only way to deal with darkness was with aggression.

The macho model for dealing with darkness goes beyond confident praying to being abusive in ministering to the demonized. Jesus operated with great compassion and mercy with all the demonized people he met. He moved in power, but he was careful to preserve the dignity of individuals.

The macho approach puts the emphasis on the strength of the one ministering, not on the strength of God. None of us can handle that level of pressure for long. I have watched people attempt to duke it out with the powers of darkness, only to eventually become overwhelmed and drop out. Over time, I have discovered a balance in my approach to doing warfare that works over the long haul: the mellow way.

The Mellow: *"Darkness scatters in the presence of light."* While the meek, manic, and macho approaches focus on darkness, the mellow approach focuses on God. Our goal is to bring the light of God to shine on the effects of darkness wherever we find it.

Jesus was light-focused in battling darkness. He came to our spiritually darkened planet with a simple agenda: to penetrate darkness of every kind with the light of God's kingdom. Jesus modeled a subtle confidence in the power of God. He was relaxed, nearly nonchalant in dealing with the demonic, because he knew from experience that "greater is he who is in you than he who is in the world" (1 Jn 4:4). He was aggressive when needed, but his strategy emphasized the power of God, not humankind.

A simple match when struck chases away darkness. In a cave a mere ten-watt lamp is visible for hundreds of feet. That's what Jesus was getting at when he said, "I have come as a light into the world, that whoever believes in me should not abide in darkness" (Jn 12:46). His approach was simple: *Turn on the light and darkness will flee.*

The power of this truth hit me one summer when I worked in a copper mine in Arizona. My job was to carry dynamite and blasting caps from underground storage areas to the miners. Most of the summer I worked at 5,000 feet; that is, just short of one mile straight down. From the time I descended into the darkness until the end of the shift, the only light I saw was provided by my helmet lamp and the battery pack on my work belt. I had never seen total darkness until that summer.

◆◆◆

His approach was simple:
Turn on the light and darkness will flee.

◆◆◆

The Apostle John declares that Jesus came into a world of spiritual darkness to shine the light of the life of God (see John 1:4, 5). Spiritually speaking, the world apart from God is at the 5,000-foot level of a copper mine. Jesus came to bring the light of God into the utter darkness of this world. We may try many methods to drive away darkness, but only one works. Like Jesus, we must usher the light of God into a world stuck at 5,000 feet.

I was able to shine the light of God's love into significant darkness recently while cleaning toilets with a pastor in the Dallas area. We entered an Islamic grocery market and offered to clean the toilets to show God's love in a practical way. The manager surprised me by firing back in a Middle-Eastern accent, "We have twelve toilets. If you want to show me the love of Jesus, you can start by cleaning all twelve!" I've cleaned as many as three commodes at a business, but twelve would take an hour or more.

"How about three toilets? We have more places to clean later."

He wouldn't budge. "If you won't clean all twelve, don't bother cleaning any of them."

I could see my toilet negotiating was getting me nowhere, so I gave in; but as we walked back to the bathroom he shifted gears. "You know, we really have only two toilets. I told you twelve because I was giving you a test to see if you were for real."

Apparently I passed the test because as we cleaned, each of the dozen or so employees came back to talk to us one by one. Each asked, "Why are you doing this?" I don't know how many opportunities they'd had to interact with Christians, but as I walked out of that store, I felt as though I'd shined the light of God into some regions that had never seen even a flicker.

WHEN IS WARFARE INEFFECTIVE?

The last piece of therapeutic advice Bobo needed was to stop chasing those cotton-pickin' rabbits. A natural follow-up to pet counseling could be pet recovery groups. Bobo could have used an RA group: Rabbits Anonymous.

As Christians we have our own version of the rabbit chase that keeps us from being effective: We go off on tangents. These usually start out as legitimate attempts to correct an area of weakness in the church. In my twenty-plus years as a Christian, however, I have seen many well-intentioned movements become over-emphasized. Some of these include:

- the hyper-faith tangent
- the inner-healing tangent
- the King-James-Bible-only tangent
- the praying-for-one-hour tangent
- the return-to-liturgy tangent.

If imbalances like these are a problem, those connected with spiritual warfare take the cake, literally.

My friend Joanie had the bad fortune to be in a small group during a demon-hunting tangent that swept through churches in Southern California. She requested prayer from the group for strength to resist eating foods that weren't good for her. She was especially fond of chocolate cake. As the group members prayed, one person had a "word from the Lord" that the root of Joanie's problem was not human weakness, but an actual demon of chocolate cake! She was a good sport and let them pray for her, but her problem was eventually corrected through Weight Watchers, not through the removal of evil spirits.

Every tangent I've encountered contains a kernel of forgotten wisdom we probably ought to incorporate into our walk with Christ. But each of these becomes toxic when pursued apart from the greater purpose of God for the church. Jesus has called us to travel a specific road: We are to change the world's views about God.

HOW TO AVOID RABBIT-TRAIL CHRISTIANITY

In his book *Church Planting for a Greater Harvest,*[2] Peter Wagner points out that when Christian movements stop seeking to win others to Christ they stop growing, become stale, lose money, and begin to die. Billy Graham believes we will share a major regret when we finish this life: "I wish I had allowed my life to count more for bringing others to Christ."[3]

I agree. There will always be yet another movement that promises to be a "work of God." To avoid the tragedy of finishing life only to realize we pursued the next thing but not the main thing, we need to take a few simple steps.

Value the leadership of God's Word. To engage in authentic spiritual warfare, by bringing light to darkened eyes, we need to anchor ourselves upon God's unchanging Word. We must return to God through his Word daily and pray, "I open my heart to you and your truth, dear God. Mold me with your Word more than any force I will encounter today."

Value depth in Christ. Jesus gave us simple instructions: "Love the Lord your God with all your heart and with all your soul and with all your mind" (Mt 22:37). The imagery Jesus used in the parable of the sower and the seed to describe the shallow soil (see

Matthew 13) illustrates the person caught up in tangential Christianity. This plant had a root that was constantly looking for depth. It was constantly on a search for something to sink its roots into, but it was continually frustrated because it sought depth in shallow places that could never satisfy.

Similarly, those who are planting their lives in anything other than a desire to love God are living in shallow soil. Without adequate depth they will come up short in fully loving God, and thus they will never be able to bear the fruit of fulfilling Jesus' commandment, "Love your neighbor as yourself" (Mt 22:39). For an accurate reading on how you're doing, ask yourself daily, "Did I grow in my love for God today? Did I love people more today?" Truly "deep" Christians are those who know they are accepted and loved by God. Out of the overflow of that security and joy they are able to give away the love of God.

Value people more than tasks. For several years I have been undergoing a transformation from being accomplishment-focused to people-focused. When I first came to Christ, I had a keen awareness of the "lostness" of people. Sometimes I was overwhelmed by an acute awareness of hell. I'm embarrassed to admit it, but I became so burdened with the lost condition of others that I asked God to release me from this awareness. He did, and for fifteen years I seldom thought about hell.

◆◆◆

Every tangent... becomes toxic when pursued apart from the greater purpose of God for the church.

◆◆◆

Recently God has been speaking to me and increasing my concern for those without knowledge of Christ. In Matthew 9 and 10, Jesus calls the lost "sheep without a shepherd." A sheep without a shepherd is a sheep whose days are numbered. I'm convinced that we must have Jesus' view of the lost or we will be of only limited usefulness to God. We must see those who don't know Christ as the walking dead or we will be destined for tangents, and spiritual warfare won't be practiced in the church.

I believe that those most powerfully used by God have the ability to see others as God sees them, free of facades. Dan is one of those people. A few years ago Dan left the staff of the Vineyard to plant a church outside the Cincinnati area. I didn't have high expectations for this new church to do well, but my lack of faith didn't deter Dan. I tried to adjust his expectations before he left, but he launched out with great enthusiasm just the same.

In the four years since he left, Dan has grown this new church from zero to over 600. I admit I was both thrilled about his success and curious about his "secret." His answer was simple: "I don't have any big secret except that I pray the same prayer every day: 'Lord, don't let a single person in Dayton go into eternity without knowing you.'"

"But Dan," I said, "that isn't a biblical prayer. Scripture says that some will be lost."

"Oh, I know what Scripture says. Tragically, many *will* be lost in the end, but at least that prayer pleases the heart of the Lord."

I've been praying that prayer a lot lately for the people of Cincinnati.

Pair and Share Questions

1. Has any concept you've read about so far "tilted" you? Explain.

2. Which strategy best describes your past or present encounters with spiritual darkness: Meek, Manic, Macho, or Mellow?

3. Why do you think the majority of Christians see so little evangelistic fruit in their lives?

4. What do you think is the ultimate goal of servant warfare?

5. Do you agree that the primary task we've been given is evangelism? Why or why not?

6. Brainstorm on an act of kindness that would be a unique fit for your community. Take responsibility to carry it out.

7. Read and meditate on the truths of Matthew 9 and 10 for a week, then report your thoughts to your group.

THREE TRUTHS
THAT EMPOWER

Courage is doing what you are afraid to do.
There can be no courage unless you're scared.
— Eddie Rickenbacker —

In the days before traffic lights were common, the police used to direct traffic in major cities. Once when the police in South Africa went on strike, the traffic during rush hour was constantly gridlocked.

While trying to drive home one night, a Boy Scout leader had a bright idea: "Why don't we empower our scouts as surrogate policemen!" The plan, though unorthodox, sounded good to desperate police chiefs around the country. Within a week, several thousand scouts were given a crash course on directing traffic, and were then deputized and unleashed upon their cities. Each was issued just the essential equipment every traffic cop needs: a pair of white gloves and a loud whistle. Drivers found it odd to take orders from twelve- and thirteen-year-olds, but they quickly got used to it. With no pistol, no training, and no salary, the scouts seemed to do as well as the police. In the words of one motorist, the boys were *simply effective*. They were enabled to untangle traffic jams because they were adequately equipped for the task.

We need a similar enabling if we are to be effective in servant warfare. Fortunately, God has already fully equipped each of us with exactly the same tools Jesus used to accomplish the job: power, authority, and peace. Like the Boy Scouts demonstrated, it doesn't take a lot of equipment to be effective.

FULLY EQUIPPED

In my experience in the charismatic wing of the church, I've seen many people who are looking for an outward experience to equip them: things like being slain in the Spirit or speaking in tongues. While I have benefited from these kinds of experiences, they are only part of the picture. More important is settling some fundamental questions.

In John 13, Jesus came face to face with the most traumatic spiritual crisis of his life. Ironically, on the evening of his greatest need for power Jesus had the fewest external resources. He was facing death. He was about to bear the sin of the world on the cross. For three years he had poured his life into twelve people, yet one would betray him that night.

◆◆◆

Jesus approached gaining authority a lot like the Boy Scouts in South Africa: His wasn't an external empowering, but an internal permission-giving.

◆◆◆

Jesus, however, was able to survive the spiritual pressure in the Garden of Gethsemane and the abuse of his trial, and remain faithful to his mission: to go to the cross. Jesus approached gaining authority a lot like the Boy Scouts in South Africa: His wasn't an external empowering, but an internal permission-giving. He had settled some basic questions about his origin, purpose in life, and destiny.

Where do I come from?
Why am I here?
Where am I going?

If you were to take a Philosophy 101 course, these would be called the *basic existential questions* because we all instinctively ask these about our life. Until they are answered, we find it impossible to be completely at peace. They are at the root of all identity problems we face and the basis of most counseling sessions. If we are to launch out in power and authority we must ask and answer the same questions Jesus did.

Jesus knew he had come from God, that he was sent by the Father to bring the kingdom to earth, and that he would return to God. This knowledge empowered him to step beyond himself and serve others: "So he got up from the meal, took off his outer clothing, and wrapped a towel around his waist. After that, he poured water into a basin and began to wash his disciples' feet, drying them with the towel that was wrapped around him" (Jn 13:4).

As believers in Christ we have the same information Jesus had. We know where we're from, what we're for, and where we're going. All the tools we need have been given to us. We don't need to get something else before we can be effective. Peter states that we have "everything we need" (2 Pt 1:3). We can settle the big questions those outside of Christ can't answer. We can be at rest and empowered to live like Jesus in this world: as servants doing the will of the Father.

"Where do I come from?" "Jesus knew… that he had come from God" (Jn 13:3). Jesus had settled the question of his past. He was aware that he had been sent by the Father to bring the kingdom of God to earth. That understanding provided him with an essential view of life each of us must have if we are to make a difference. We must realize that we, too, have been sent by God, and he has given us the legal right to represent his kingdom.

Jesus didn't come to earth after having a bright idea one day. There was no "Save the Humans" committee formed to deputize him. He was sent by his Father who decided, "I am sending you to earth to bring my love to this rebellious planet. My hand will rest upon you as you go because I send you to do my bidding." Though Jesus was fully God, he walked the earth as a human being. He needed the authority of heaven in order to make a difference in this mortal world.

◆◆◆

We, too, have been sent by God,
and he has given us the legal right
to represent his kingdom.

◆◆◆

Every follower of Jesus Christ has the same authority available in his or her life, but not every believer wields the same amount. In fact, I have found that the greatest levels of authority are often demonstrated by the most unlikely people. Jesus himself must have appeared an unlikely candidate to wield the authority of God. For example, when he met up with the demonized man of Gerasenes (see Luke 8:26-39), he certainly wasn't at his physical best. After a night of trying to sleep through a rough storm, he was tired, dirty, and hungry. But that is when he crossed paths with the most severely demonized person mentioned in the New Testament. This man was so captivated by darkness he lived naked among the graves. Yet when Jesus met him, the power and authority of God liberated the man on the spot. Fatigue and less than ideal circumstances didn't affect the outcome because Jesus knew that he'd been sent by God to do the work of the kingdom.

Seventy-four-year-old Helen is another unlikely carrier of God's authority. For years she has had a ministry to the addicted, hurting, and broken in the University District of Seattle. This part of town is considered unsafe for anyone at night, so it's especially odd to see an elderly woman walking around at midnight with her purse slung over her shoulder. An easy target for muggers, you say? That's exactly the idea.

In the beginning Helen walked the streets with a Bible and gospel tracts in hand but had little luck gaining an audience with the locals. More often than not, her purse was stolen as she made her rounds. After losing a dozen purses she changed tactics. Now she buys a batch of the least expensive purses available at the thrift store. Inside her cheap purse she places a couple of dollars and a little note that reads:

"My dear friend, you must be in great trouble if you needed to steal this purse. I am sorry for you and I love you. I also believe God loves you and wants to help you. So do I! Here is my phone number and address. Please come see me."[1]

◆◆◆

Knowing that God has sent her is what makes Helen fruitful in this unique ministry.

◆◆◆

Now I don't recommended this approach! But the idea of letting muggers take her purse was God's, not Helen's. She isn't carrying out her agenda, but the agenda of the Father who sent her to do his bidding. Several years ago she felt the Lord gave her this idea as she prayed for the University District. She ran the idea past mature Christian friends and leaders in her life, and after much prayerful consideration, all agreed the idea was worth a try. Over the years she has not only been protected, but she has also been fruitful. The numerous articles about her in local newspapers have shaped the public's view of the church. Knowing that God has sent her is what makes Helen fruitful in this unique ministry.

Sometimes Christians think they have to do something to gain authority instead of realizing that power and authority have already been given to them. One of the attempts to gain authority is the large rallies that have become popular in many cities across the US. Having attended a number of these, it seems many of them have a pep meeting feel to them. The understanding seems to be, "As we rally all the Christians of the city, we will take authority over the powers of darkness." I appreciate the unifying effect these gatherings have on local churches, but often I hear preachers talking to those already converted.

What if these rallies became more practical by using the authority we already have and aiming that toward serving the city? That's exactly what some friends and I did at a recent large rally in downtown Cincinnati. As thousands of Christians waved banners and preachers spoke over a PA system, about a dozen of us washed several hundred windshields and gave out frozen popsicles to overheated downtowners.

◆◆◆

As we step out in faith and begin to serve,
we will see the authority of the Father
come upon our lives.

◆◆◆

The highlight of our outreach was a panicky looking man standing over his wife who was slumped on a park bench. His wife had collapsed with a diabetic attack and needed something sweet immediately. He was in a quandary: There was a snack shop across the park, but he didn't want to leave his wife's side. Of course, we were thrilled to give her a popsicle. As she finished and began to feel better, the man with tears in his eyes thanked the team, saying, "I don't know what I would have done if you hadn't come along when you did."

Some might ask, "What good will a popsicle do in the scope of things?" A popsicle alone may not be much, but that same popsicle given with the authority of the Kingdom of God will make a difference every time. My guess is that man and his wife will never forget that particular popsicle. They will remember the people God sent who said, "We just want to show you God's love in a practical way." As we realize we've been sent by God, we don't need to argue our position. As we step out in faith and begin to serve, we will see the authority of the Father come upon our lives.

"Why am I here?" Jesus understood his purpose. He said he came "not... to do my will but to do the will of him who sent me" (Jn 6:38). As Jesus obeyed the Father and stepped out to do his will, the power and authority of God came through his life. Whether by teaching or healing or feeding or walking on water, Jesus acted on behalf of his Father.

We often miss the point that we have exactly the same purpose in life: to do God's will. That's why we're not taken directly to heaven the moment we're saved through Christ. When we set out to do the will of God, the same power and authority that Jesus demonstrated flow through us.

The members of a Methodist prayer group in Texas are finding this to be true. As they go door-to-door throughout their community they simply ask residents, "May we pray for you?" One family might need prayer for a financial need. The next person might need physical healing. Whatever the need, it is lifted up to the Lord. When the prayers are answered, the people connect the change with the presence and love of God. Usually it isn't long before they move toward Christ.

At one home the prayer group knew something was up when the family just looked at each other with a blank stare and said, "Well, you could pray for Sis." The group found Sis lying on a sofa. She was a teenager, but she looked more like a death camp survivor. She was so anorexic she was in danger of losing her life. Her family explained that she'd been in and out of hospitals and clinics but had found nothing that worked to keep her at an adequate weight. The doctors didn't know what else to do.

The prayer team didn't know much about Sis' medical condition, but they did know how to pray. As they prayed that day they saw some response in her. They came back the next day, and the next and the next. After two weeks of daily prayer therapy, Sis began to show obvious signs of recovery. During week three, the entire family was convinced of the reality and love of God and they all received Christ. That was three years ago. Sis is in college now and has no symptoms of her former condition.

D. John Richard of the Evangelical Fellowship of Asia in New Delhi, India, says it well:

> All our planning of strategies for evangelizing the unreached will be unproductive, if the twin strategies of prayer and love are not given the due place they deserve. It is in these twin areas that the church around the world is woefully lacking. We know so little of what it means "to advance on our knees" and to reflect the compassionate heart of Christ in our daily dealings. There's no getting away from the fact that the only argument to which a person will succumb is that of love being piled on him. People gravitate to where love is. "The kingdom of God is not in word, but in power." Not in words piled upon words, but in power over unconcern and indifference, power over self-centeredness and self-love.[2]

"Where am I going?" Jesus had perspective. The night before he died was no doubt the most spiritually trying time of his life. At some level, he must have been feeling, "Am I in this all alone?" But in spite of the chaos of the evening, Jesus operated in absolute peace. John tells us, "Jesus knew... that he was returning to God" (Jn 13:3). The knowledge that his Father was at work in the midst of chaos gave Jesus an essential commodity for effectiveness: *peace*.

My friends Rich and Cindy work in San Francisco as vocalists in an opera company. When they met their new next-door apartment neighbor in the Haight District not long ago, they knew they'd met their match. Shirley seemed nice until she saw the fish symbol on their door and asked, "You two aren't Christians, are you?"

"Yes, we are. Are you a believer, too?"

"I am a believer, but in Satan."

For a moment they thought she was joking, but over the next few weeks Shirley's dark faith became anything but a laughing matter. The next day she began leaving a daily curse on their doorstep. Rich confided in me, "It's a bit intimidating to find animal parts lying on your doorstep every morning."

As servant warriors, they chose not only to pray for themselves and for Shirley, but also to get some weapons ready. They fired up the oven and began to bake chocolate-chip cookies for Shirley. The other neighbors thought it was an odd sight: Shirley putting curses on Rich and Cindy, and them baking cookies for her.

It wasn't long before Shirley broke emotionally and spiritually. Rich and Cindy received a touching letter in which Shirley shared, "I've never met people like you. If you are what this Jesus stuff is about, I'm interested." They told me later, "The entire time Shirley was next door, we felt the deep peace of God in spite of her bizarre actions."

◆◆◆

"If you are what this Jesus stuff is about,
I'm interested."

◆◆◆

Since the church began, Christians have lived valiant lives against staggering odds because they've had great security knowing they were part of the family of God. As we realize that some day soon we will be with him forever, we are empowered. That understanding makes us more than survivors in this world, no matter what level of darkness we face.

HOW TO ACCESS GOD'S POWER

Our greatest danger as messengers of God's kingdom is becoming overwhelmed with our task. I find it encouraging to reflect on the principles by which Jesus lived—simple truths that gave him confidence to do the assignments of the day, no matter what the circumstances.

Expect God to work. Jesus rose every day to do the will of his Father. Do you think he started each morning with the thought, "Today I face the hordes of darkness—just me against the myriad powers that stand against me," followed by a reluctant, wavering stumble into the day? Hardly. Jesus understood that it's God's power that makes all things possible. God was with Jesus as Jesus did God's will. He is with us in exactly the same way. So step out in faith and exercise the authority God has given you.

Expect the Father's power, not yours. We all have problems trusting God. J.B. Phillips, in his timeless book *Your God is Too Small*,[3] says we have many false pictures of God. Most of those images result from our thinking erroneously that God is a lot like us. We begin to picture him as being stuck in the stuff of life just like we are.

Theologians speak of God as being *transcendent;* that is, he stands on the outside of our problems, unaffected by the things that burden us. Though he is with us by the presence of the Holy Spirit, he is never bogged down, and his authority is constantly available to us.

Notice what God is doing. Jesus allowed his *Father* to set his agenda. He shared one of the secrets to his success when he said, "Whatever the Father does the Son also does" (Jn 5:19). When we are doing what God wants us to do, we can count on him to open a path for us that only he can open.

Recognize your assignment. Jesus understood his specific call and he stayed focused on it so that when he died he was able to say, "It is finished." In other words, "Mission accomplished." Many were healed through Jesus' life and many demons were expelled, but when he said his work was finished there were still people who needed healing. Clearly, Jesus wasn't on this earth to cast out every demon and heal all the sick. He was here to live among us, to show us God's love and power, and to enable us to be reconciled to God. That was his mission, and once it was accomplished, he returned to the Father.

When we know what God wants of us, we don't need to take responsibility for every conceivable assignment. You and I individually cannot reach everyone. God has an assignment in mind that only you can do. Focus on it and complete it well.

Hang in there when the going gets tough. The Bible often speaks of our need to persevere, as in the passage, "He said this so that we would always pray and never give up" (Lk 18:1). The Apostle Paul also offered metaphors about hanging tough and finishing the race (see 1 Corinthians 9:24; 2 Timothy 4:7).

One of the primary tactics of the enemy is to get Christians to believe that no matter what we do, our actions are futile and useless. The truth is, God is changing the world through us, whether we recognize it or not. The best and most lasting fruit of my life so far has matured in me during phases of ministry when I was convinced that little or nothing was happening.

Rest in the strength of God. We live in his strength, not our own. The way into the Christian life is also the way onward. We came to Christ clinging to him for our salvation and for right standing with God. Now we must depend on God's strength as we go forward.

For years I have tried to live by the motto, "Unless God shows up, I am in big trouble." The good news is that God shows up willingly, instantly. And he will show up for all our days. With the strength of God in our lives, every obstacle pales by comparison, no matter how much power the opposition appears to have. It's been said, "It doesn't matter if we're facing a housefly or an

African elephant in the spiritual realm. In the presence of an atom bomb, the same thing happens to both of them."

Be available and step out in obedience. Authority came to Jesus in increasing measure as he gave away the kingdom. It is human nature to reason, "When I get well, when I can afford it, when I'm adequately trained, *then* I'll begin to give of myself." That isn't the way Jesus ran things with the apostles. Time and again he sent them to do his bidding with little or no training, yet the results were historic. As they were willing to follow his direction in spite of lingering questions, their fears were replaced with confidence in a great God.

We need to develop the attitude of *"whatever, Lord,"* a willingness to do the *next thing* God places before us. As we walk in this perspective the authority and power of God flows constantly through us and the world is changed.

◆◆◆

*We need to develop the attitude of
"whatever, Lord," a willingness to
do the next thing God places before us.*

◆◆◆

Singer-songwriter Keith Green captured this attitude twenty years ago when he said to a concert crowd, "If you take the words 'go' and 'do' out of the Bible, the rest of the book doesn't make sense. It becomes a huge Hallmark card: kind of nice, cozy, and syrupy-sweet, but completely without power." If we take the wait-until-I-get-touched approach, I predict we will wait—and waste—a lifetime. Now is the time to step out and look for the next small thing the Lord has for us to do.

A group of Christians in Toledo stepped out in just this way at a recent rock concert. The managers of a local Christian radio station decided to sponsor an outreach at the Nine Inch Nails concert. This band is one of the darkest alternative rock bands. They sing of the meaninglessness of life and typically destroy their equipment at the end of their shows.

The station sent out a "calling all servants" plea and about 100 Christians showed up to give away soft drinks, coffee, and hot chocolate to incoming concert-goers. They were able to directly touch some 600 young people with God's love. The highlight of the night came when the band's limo pulled up and asked, "What are you Christians doing here?" As they passed a case of pop through the limo window along with some follow-up cards they said, "You might say we're trying to make Toledo holy." To that the band said, "That's cool!"

◆◆◆

"You might say we're trying to make Toledo holy."

◆◆◆

The story of this outreach captured the attention of the local church community. For weeks Christians asked, "A Coke and Nine Inch Nails? Go figure!" The account was written up in the local paper, released onto the Associated Press wire service, and appeared in dozens of papers across the US.[4]

As we do a small thing, God's life will flow through us. Helen "the purse lady," Rich and Cindy with their Satanist neighbor, Toledo folks offering soft drinks to alternative rockers: They are all ordinary people who know where they're from, what they're here for, and where they're going. Because they are available to do the will of their Father, they are making a difference in their world.

Pair and Share Questions

1. Considering where you are in your life, how would you answer the following questions:

   Where do I come from?

Why am I here?

Where am I going?

2. Explain what gives the average person the legal right (or authority) to represent the kingdom of God on earth.

3. Discuss several ways in which people try to gain authority in God's kingdom through their own endeavors.

4. Share stories of people you've known who you believe have done the Father's will.

5. Describe a situation in which you knew you were sent by God to do something, and that knowledge made all the difference in the outcome.

6. What challenge are you facing that would be easier to deal with if God's authority was upon your life?

7. God has a plan for changing the world and only you can do your part. Write down three steps you can take to start implementing God's plan.

8. At the end of your life, do you feel you'll be able to say as Jesus did, "Mission accomplished!"? Why or why not?

9. In the week ahead, cultivate an attitude of willingness to do the next thing God places before you. Note these experiences and share them with your group.

CHANGING SPIRITUAL CLIMATES

The course of human history is determined,
not by what happens in the skies, but by
what takes place in our hearts.
— Sir Arthur Keith —

Since writing *Conspiracy of Kindness*, I have done dozens of radio interviews with stations across the US. Surprisingly, the best radio experience I've had was on a secular station in the Cincinnati area. It is the strongest power output station in the region and reaches over thirty states and Eastern Canada with talk radio.

I'd listened to the station enough to know a bit of what I was up against. Fully expecting some ultra-left, or far-right-wing callers to give me the third degree, I came prepared with a sheet full of great one-liners in hopes of holding my own with whomever might call.

The show host summarized the thinking behind using serving projects to connect with people who don't yet know Christ. After a few minutes he opened up the phone lines for responses. I was a little concerned when the lines quickly filled with callers, but my fear gave way to astonishment when the callers began to recount stories of how kindness projects our church had done had touched their lives. Not only were they not critical, but they wanted to let me know how much they appreciated being served. Most of the callers started out with, "I don't go to church, but...." then continued with how our acts of service pierced their hearts. Several asked for our address so they could give a donation. When I said we wouldn't take their money, they were clearly moved.

The best call came near the end of the show when a businessman on a cellular phone disclosed, "There I was downtown running to my car, fully expecting a parking ticket. Instead of a ticket there was a card that read, 'Your parking meter looked hungry, so we fed it!'" He went on, "I stood there stunned. My first thought was, 'I don't deserve this.' I should have gotten a parking ticket, but instead I got love."

After a pregnant pause on live radio I said, "That's exactly the point, sir. You probably did deserve a ticket, but we extended a bit of grace to you in the form of a dime in your meter and a card explaining what we did. In exactly the same way, Jesus Christ has extended his love and grace to each of us, even though not a single one of us deserves it."

◆◆◆

> *"I don't deserve this. I should have gotten a parking ticket, but instead I got love."*

◆◆◆

Radio is supposed to be a one-way communication device, but that day I could almost hear thousands of spiritual powers being dethroned as the power of kindness struck a blow. My eyes were opened to the way the atmosphere in our city has changed over the past few years as we've served tens of thousands in practical ways. I didn't get to use even one of my clever comeback lines, but I did learn an important lesson: Sometimes the most effective spiritual battles are waged not with might, but with service. Our best weapon is not raw force, but simple, powerful kindness.

POWERFUL KINDNESS?

Our culture seems to like paradoxes. Consider the name of the 1960s rock group, Iron Butterfly. Or the song writer whose aunt, who raised him, wasn't keen on his plan to be a musician. To drive home her point, she gave her fourteen-year-old nephew a ceramic plaque made in the shape of a guitar with an inscription underneath: "You'll never make any money playing that guitar." John Lennon held on to that plaque as a reminder of the irony of his career. When he died in 1980, Lennon had earned more than any musician-writer of this century.[1]

Rock music doesn't have the corner on paradoxes; in fact, the best oxymorons are found in the Bible. For example,

- "Love your enemy" (Mt 5:44).

- "When struck on the cheek, turn your other cheek also" (Mt 5:39).

- "The first shall be last" (Mt 19:30).

- "If someone wants… your tunic, let him have your cloak as well" (Mt 5:40).

- "If someone forces you to go one mile, go with him two miles" (Mt 5:41).

If the kingdom of God is based on the power of love, servanthood, and kindness, why do Christians try to fight fire with fire? God has entrusted the weapon of kindness to the church, but few of us think of power when we ponder kindness. Kindness may even seem a bit schmaltzy to us. We may think of Mr. Rogers in the cardigan sweater his mother knitted for him, smiling as he slips on his blue gym shoes and asks us, "Won't you be my neighbor?"

Is kindness corny? Perhaps in certain settings it is, but not when it's delivered by a follower of Jesus Christ. When a Christian uses the tool of kindness, it has the power to radically alter the human heart.

A local Christian radio manager called me to arrange for an interview about serving projects. I agreed to the interview, but insisted that first he tag along with me and a kindness team. We gave him the option of washing windshields, feeding parking meters, or cleaning toilets. In spite of the red power-tie he sported, he opted for the commode crew. We thought we'd have some fun with him so we didn't warn him of the dangers of dipping one's tie into the toilet. After the first stop Roy had a wet tie to remind him of his newcomer status.

The highlight of that outreach was in a beauty salon. Typically the offer to clean toilets for free is enough to shut down all conversation in a business, but this time the manager said when we were finished, "You know, this can be a pretty depressing place. These women come in here every week to get their hair done, but mostly they come to gossip and complain to one another about how hard life is. When you guys came in here it was like a fresh breeze blew through here and the tone of the place changed. Thanks for cleaning our johns, but even more, thanks for changing the mood of this place!"

Later when Roy and I were talking on the radio he admitted, "When that lady said what she did, I knew we'd made a lasting impression on each heart in that salon." Tears came to Roy's eyes as he shared that story. I knew God had done something remarkable in the heart of both the served and the servant.

GOD'S CLIMATE-CHANGERS

Just as we experience various climates in the earthly realm—heat or cold, dry or moist, bright or cloudy—similar climates exist in

the spiritual world as well. We tend to ⌐
about our business, but there is a spirit
where we go and in every encounter w

No matter what the spiritual atm
climate-changers in the world. One of ol
party at a low-income housing development, is
The prevailing spiritual climate in these apartment citie.
mistrust. We alter the spiritual climate as we invite several hu.
folks to a lunch of grilled hot dogs and hamburgers. We ofte.
games for kids, good music, and a lot of love. We usually cap off
the day by cleaning up broken glass from the playground and
installing new playground equipment. Not only do the residents
experience God's love in a practical way, but a new spiritual atmosphere is created by the power of God's kindness.

◆◆◆

"If you really want to help some folks in
need, go to the Death House."

◆◆◆

A pastor friend of mine in Orange County, California has begun
to change negative spiritual climates by using the weapon of kindness to change the neighborhoods around him. Recently while he
and a team were giving away groceries to the needy, someone suggested, "If you really want to help some folks in need, go to the
Death House." He knocked on the door of a dilapidated house
and was greeted by a long-haired biker who was dressed completely in black. This guy was thankful for the groceries, and began to
share about how he was disabled because of his past drug use. In
fact, everyone living there was receiving welfare payments.

Before long, this grateful man took the team on a tour of the
place. The house was dark, dirty, and small, yet eleven people lived
there. Everyone in the house wore only black, and they had all
dyed their hair black. The other residents were hesitant to come
near the Christians. The last part of the tour was the "death

dark, dusty room filled with evil pictures and occult Over the door was a large pentagram. As they left, this f servant warriors could tell they were being scoped out by esidents of the Death House to see if they would show them e or judgment. Apparently they passed the test, because they ere invited back. In the following weeks they fought resistance with many practical expressions of love. The residents began to ask questions about God. The head couple in the house had lived together for years, but asked, "Does the Bible say anything about marriage? We've talked about maybe getting married some day." After getting answers to their questions they asked, "Do you think your pastor could marry us?"

The last I heard, the atmosphere in that home was changing rapidly. The death room has been cleaned up and repainted white! My pastor friend said, "Pretty soon they'll have to call it the Life House. Everyone there is coming to church now. The couple is getting married soon, and the church is paying for catering to serve all their friends." The spiritual winds are shifting in one part of Orange County.

KINDNESS, OR JUST NICENESS?

Over the past five years I have trained approximately 40,000 pastors and leaders in the practice of serving their cities. When talking about the surprising dynamic of kindness I often run into skeptics. With crossed arms the not-yet-converted-to-kindness ask, "Isn't this just organized 'niceness'? How is what you're doing so different from the good deeds of the Kiwanis, Boy Scouts, or Campfire Girls?" A clear definition of kindness can clear up a lot of confusion.

The kindness I'm talking about is *practical acts of mercy done by followers of Jesus who are inspired by the Holy Spirit to see others through the eyes of God.* Paul writes that "the kindness of God leads us to repentance" (Rom 2:4). The Bible seems to distinguish between the divine quality of kindness and the human quality of niceness. In short, if kindness originates in the heart of God, then only Christians have the ability to be kind in the biblical sense of the word.

Paul lists kindness as one of the hallmarks of a person filled with the Spirit of God (see Galatians 5:22). Even the Webster's Dictionary definition of kindness implies that it's a quality found only in the spiritual realm by describing it as "having a sympathetic, helpful... forbearing nature."[2] I find it interesting that the word *forbearance* is used in that definition because Paul exhorts the Philippian believers to let their forbearing spirits be known to all men (see Philippians 4:5, NASB). Forbearance is the ability to view and love people as God sees and loves them.

If only Christians can show biblical kindness, then what do we call the benevolence that humans show on occasion? When we speak of humans who don't know Christ as being *kind*, perhaps we would be more accurate to call them *nice*. "Random acts of kindness" could be more accurately termed "random acts of *niceness*" because they are not based on the power of God. Niceness is a fickle human quality that strikes almost everyone occasionally. Non-Christian people raise billions of dollars each year for shelters for the homeless, food for the hungry, and programs for drug addicts. A friend of mine who is a regional leader with the Salvation Army told me that the majority of their budget each year is donated by shoppers in the six weeks between Thanksgiving and Christmas. Giving to the needy is something that even completely unchurched people do on occasion, but the fact is, they are demonstrating human niceness, not kindness.

Oprah Winfrey has done a number of shows on the topic of "random acts of kindness." During the planning of those shows the producers called me and said they had read my book and wondered if I'd be a guest on an upcoming show. I explained that what we do isn't based on our desire to be nice, but to show the kindness and love of God. "We are filled with God's Spirit and do acts of kindness in order to show people the reality of God and hopefully bring them to Christ. As we are kind in the name of Jesus Christ, those we serve open their hearts to a relationship with God." The producer's response? "Interesting… we'll get back to you on that!" That was eighteen months ago and I'm still waiting for the call!

Why have books such as *Random Acts of Kindness* sold like hotcakes in recent years? Because in this age of rage, niceness is news! But niceness is a world away from the kindness of God that flows through the life of a Christian.

IF KINDNESS IS SO WONDERFUL, HOW HAVE WE MISSED IT?

In our quest to find the fastest, the strongest, the superlative in every aspect of church life we have stirred up a lot of smoke, but not much fire. Why have we overlooked one of the most powerful forces right under our noses?

Kindness isn't *fast*. And it isn't flashy or impressive on the surface. Kindness seems odd because it's the tortoise approach in the age of the hare. In America in particular, we are enamored with the fast, the big, and the spectacular.

Kindness isn't *easy*. Kindness isn't a warm feeling in one's heart, it's a practical action. Because it takes time and energy to be kind, we find it difficult to actually go beyond our feelings of benevolence to take action. Most of our schedules are maxed out already, so adding even a small thing may seem overwhelming.

Kindness isn't *ego-building*. I was with a pastor recently on a toilet-cleaning expedition to local businesses. With our yellow rubber gloves on we both looked slightly less pastoral than on a typical Sunday morning. He made the comment, "When I was taking homiletics classes in seminary, I had no idea I was being prepared for this!"

Sometimes Christians, and pastors in particular, make the mistake of thinking that God is desperately counting on us to get his point across. We've all read Paul's words, "How will they hear without a preacher?" (Rom 10:14). While the gospel does have to be proclaimed to the world if we hope to change it, we are prone to overemphasize our role and underemphasize God's. I have found there is nothing like doing acts of kindness to humble us Christians and to show us how much is God's part in redeeming the world and how much (or little) is ours.

Pelagius, one of the early heretics in church history, believed that God's actions are limited to the actions of his people. It was determined by early church councils that Pelagius, a British monk, was limiting God by focusing too much on people's part in redemption.

◆◆◆

I haven't been to your church, but I've sent three friends who loved your Sunday celebration.

◆◆◆

Recently a toilet-cleaning crew walked into a business and before they could say a word the guy in charge said, "Don't tell me, you're from the Vineyard!"

"How did you know that?" they asked.

"Well, first, *who else but you guys* would be out cleaning toilets! You've made quite an impression on me already. Two years ago at Christmas you wrapped my present at the mall. Then in May you gave me a soft drink at a traffic light. Last fall you raked my leaves. I haven't been to your church, but I've sent three friends who loved your Sunday celebration. Now they're trying to get *me* to come! I'll make it there before long." Then he said, "You know,

I've had your card on my dashboard for about two years now. I often think about you guys and God."

I was deeply humbled to hear that man's words. We had served in a small way, but God is doing a much larger work than we could have imagined.

Kindness isn't *natural*. When we come to Christ, our nature is changed by God's Spirit and we become capable of living in new ways. As his life flows through us, what was unnatural becomes natural.

My life is a good example of how this works. Those who know me best think it's ironic that I'm writing books and articles on kindness because I'm not a Mr. Rogers kind of guy. My associate pastor, Dave, is wired differently than I am, and his gifts complement my weaknesses. He is naturally very gentle and warm—one of the nicest guys you could ever meet. I will probably never be a warm fuzzy kind of person because that's not the way I'm wired emotionally, but I hope I'll be more kind and gentle because of the Holy Spirit's transforming presence in me.

Kindness isn't *easy to quantify*. In the modern church we don't feel comfortable with what is hard to measure. We like to support what can be proven effective with objective evaluations. I'm all for taking measurements to see if we're failing or succeeding, and I keep many regarding our church, but some of the most dynamic things in God's economy are tough to quantify.

Recently I spoke to a denominational gathering of pastors and was asked a common question: "What about the people you encounter who are from out of town? If you serve people at Reds baseball games where many you touch live elsewhere, how will that help your local church to grow?" I surprised the pastor who asked that question when I answered, "We aren't serving people to get them to come to our church. We're serving them to show God's love and to get our people to shift their focus outward."

When the climate of God's love and presence is evident among a group of people, spiritual barriers crumble, old ways of thinking change, and people come to see and know Jesus as he really is. Spiritual warfare isn't so much a program as it is an *atmosphere*. Our church has grown dramatically, from thirty members to three thousand in ten years. We have built our fellowship less on confronting darkness head-on than on cultivating an atmosphere of kindness and love.

◆◆◆

Spiritual warfare isn't so much a
program as it is an atmosphere.

◆◆◆

Other pastors often ask me, "How do you do it?" With pen pressed to their yellow pad they wait to record the formula for transformation in their own churches. They are usually confounded when I tell them, "Create an atmosphere of God's love and kindness in your city and you will see people come to Christ continually." While success cannot always be measured, about 1,500 people opened their hearts to Jesus Christ at our multiple weekend celebrations last year.

CREATING A NEW CLIMATE

A number of things can happen at deep, seemingly impenetrable levels of unbelievers' hearts when they experience God's kindness. Though we sometimes overlook its power, the people receiving kindness do not. It changes the climate of their hearts.

Non-Christians *respond* to kindness. Through kindness we speak a universal language that transcends many barriers. One youth leader told me some stories about his recent trip to Monterrey, Mexico with a couple dozen high-school kids dedicated to serving projects. He said that serving went a long way toward overcoming the language barriers.

"We gave away frozen popsicles with a card in Spanish," he said, "explaining what we were up to. We had only one translator, so when someone had a hot prospect going we would nab the translator. The best encounter of the trip for me was with a wild-eyed guy who ran up waving his arms and shouting angrily. He turned out to be a radical political activist who was furious that we were invading his country by pushing our religion on him. Instead of arguing—which we couldn't have done if we had wanted to—we smiled and offered him a frozen popsicle. After several popsicles, everything about this guy had changed. We didn't see him receive Christ, but we sure saw his heart turn in a different direction."

Closer to home, a college student told me of his recent adventure while raking leaves at a fraternity house. His approach is to begin raking without asking permission. "Usually the frat guys first peek out the window, then come out to ask me what I'm up to. I love to see the look on their faces when I tell them I'm not taking money, but just want to show them the love of God in a practical way."

This particular Saturday one hung-over-looking fraternity member came out to ask, "So, did you get a DUI ticket and a sentence to do community service?"

"No, I'm raking leaves to show you guys God's love in a practical way. It's for free."

The frat brother looked a bit shocked. After a moment of looking puzzled he said, "Well, could I get you a beer?" That offer may seem funny, but beneath his words the walls of this student's heart were coming down. For the next half-hour, more and more fraternity members came out to watch this strange sight: a Christian serving, no strings attached.

Non-Christians *remember* kindness. In spite of my critical, analytical bent, the more I serve my way into our community the more I'm convinced that the power of kindness can make a permanent impression on those we serve. Every week at our services I meet newcomers like Bill and Susan. They are sharp, suburban professionals. They have not received Christ, but they are openly seeking, reading, and asking questions. What drew them to the Vineyard?

"A junior-high kid gave us a Coke some time ago as we walked out of the grocery store. We'd been attending a Bible study sponsored by the Jehovah's Witnesses, but that just didn't feel right. That Coke got us talking and thinking in a different direction, and now we're here!"

Non-Christians *rehearse* their conversion when they are shown kindness. I can't prove it, but I have a feeling that prior to coming to Christ, a seeker begins to imagine himself or herself in the role of following Christ. Long before two people marry they begin to wonder, "What would it be like to be Mr. or Mrs. —— ?" They think long and hard about the implications of entering into that relationship before even talking about making a commitment. A similar mental play takes place inside the mind of a non-Christian. As that scenario is played out, internal walls of self-deception and darkness are brought down one by one.

My friend Ed was a prominent leader in the Hare Krishna movement in the 1970s. At one time these shaved-headed devotees were almost constantly posted at airports to collect funds for their group. When their international leader, Parupaba, died, Ed became disillusioned with the new leadership and left the ashram in Los Angeles to rent his own apartment.

Edith, an elderly Christian lady next door, began to show Ed the love of Christ in small ways. First she invited him over for meatloaf—not something a vegetarian can get excited about eating! But Ed started coming over to ask her probing philosophical questions about Christianity. Usually her response was, "I don't know about that, but I do know that God loves you incredibly."

Little did Edith know that Ed began to rehearse the idea of coming to Christ. He began to wonder what life would be like if he became a Christian. One day while driving down the freeway listening to Bob Dylan's first Christian album, Ed was so touched by the Spirit of God that he pulled over to the shoulder of the Santa Monica Freeway and, through sobs of repentance, he asked Christ to come into his life. Ed was "tilted" by Edith's kindness, and what he began to rehearse mentally was eventually played out.

Non-Christians *repent* **when they are shown kindness.** Paul says that "God's kindness leads us to repentance" (Rom 2:4). The Bible contains no other reference to people being led to repentance by anything other than kindness! Faith, love, mercy, and prayer are all great practices, but none of them promises to lead us to repentance.

Paul exhorted the Philippians to "let your forbearing spirit be known to all men" (Phil 4:5, NASB). Paul knew that as these Christians displayed the love of Christ to all the people around them, they would change the spiritual climate of their city.

We must never lose sight of the primary goal of spiritual warfare: to loosen the powerful grip of darkness as people are converted to Christ. Kindness is the tool for the warfare-impaired. Any average follower of Jesus Christ can be kind.

◆◆◆

*"A Jesus who mows lawns for people:
this kind of Messiah I could get interested in!"*

◆◆◆

Recently a couple of men I know decided to spend Saturday morning serving their neighborhood by mowing lawns. One lawn had particularly long grass. They discovered that a retired Jewish medical doctor lived there who was confined to a wheelchair, and was thus unable to mow his lawn. When they finished mowing, they stopped by to offer prayer to the doctor. He thanked them for the prayer and the mowing job and said, "You know, I am an old Jewish man. Not once in my life have I even thought about becoming a Christian until today. A Jesus who mows lawns for people: this kind of Messiah I could get interested in!"

They said, "We'll be back!"

An elderly Jewish man, a Hare Krishna leader, talk-radio listeners. For years I tried to reach folks like these for Christ with a mental attack. I never saw much fruit for my efforts. In fact, I just made people angry. What I didn't understand was that this is a spiritual battle that needs to be fought at a deeper, yet simpler level. God's kindness shown in practical ways accomplishes more than any fine-sounding argument or fear-based threat.

Kindness can change the climate in even the most distant heart.

Pair and Share Questions

1. Have each person in the group describe either an act of kindness done to them or one they have done to someone else. How did both the server and the served benefit?

2. Do the acts of kindness you show tend to be "hit and miss" or regular and planned?

3. Describe how you have put the powerful tool of kindness to work in the past week.

4. Before reading this chapter, had you ever thought of kindness as a weapon? What are the familiar weapons in your arsenal as a Christian?

5. What are some of the "climates" in your life? in your city? at work? at home? at church? in your neighborhood? What are some specific things you could do to become a climate-changer for God?

6. Kindness isn't fast, easy, ego-building, natural, or easy to quantify. In spite of these apparent difficulties, why is it so effective?

BINDING THE POWERS
OF DARKNESS

Give help rather than advice.
— Luc de Vauvenargues —

In spite of significant gains on the missions scene, one trend troubles missions strategists: the strong advance of Islam world-wide. I am particularly aware of the appeal of Islam because a huge mosque was recently erected down the street from me. Many trend-forecasters believe that in the next century the big challenge to Christianity will be the work of Islamic missionaries throughout the world.

This growing Islamic presence is the result of significant strategic planning. Somewhere in the Middle East is a headquarters for Islamic missions, much like the Christian world's equivalent, the US Center for World Missions in Pasadena. The president of an evangelical denomination relayed the observations of some Islamic strategists he knows. "The only missionaries we fear," they said, "are the Franciscan monks. For 700 years they have given us fits. Our approach is to persuade potential converts with apologetics. We are great at arguing, but that doesn't work with Franciscans. Instead of engaging us, they quietly go about our cities, serving everyone. Once people are served they become interested in

Christianity, and the next thing you know they've become followers of Jesus. Those Franciscan Christians don't fight fair with us!"

The Franciscans demonstrate a powerful principle when they quietly serve. They have not tried to be the smartest, or the ones who win arguments. Instead they have proven for over seven centuries that kindness is a force that defeats the powers of darkness. Because they aspire to win hearts more than discussions, God has blessed this group with evangelistic favor.

◆◆◆

*"Those Franciscan Christians
don't fight fair with us!"*

◆◆◆

Jesus spoke in Matthew 12 of the necessity to "bind" darkness as the kingdom of God goes forward upon earth. He essentially said, "Where you find darkness, bind it that the light of the kingdom might come near." But what exactly does it mean to "bind" evil forces?

UNBINDING CONFUSION

I once heard a Christian interrupt someone he disagreed with by saying, "I rebuke that, brother!" For the uninitiated, he really meant to say, "I disagree!"

Some years ago a friend disagreed with me by declaring, "I bind that!" I felt he overreacted so I fired back, "I bind your binding!" To that my friend said, "I bind your binding of my binding." That conversation escalated a bit further until we both erupted in laughter at the foolishness of what we were doing. If spiritual power really is released as we bind things, then our argument was downright mind-boggling. I suspect most Christians are about as confused about this binding thing as my friend and I were that day.

Jesus made it clear that binding is an integral part of spiritual warfare when he said, "How can anyone enter a strong man's house and carry off his possessions unless he first ties up the strong man? Then he can rob his house" (Mt 12:29, NIV). When Jesus spoke of tying up the strong man he was referring to binding darkness.

◆◆◆

If we hope to approximate the lifestyle of Jesus we must leave the safe confines of a Christians-only world.

◆◆◆

To clearly understand binding, we need to look at the original concept behind the word. Christians typically think of binding as a prayer activity, but author David Stern has a different interpretation. He writes in his *Jewish New Testament Commentary*[1] that binding is a concept rooted in Judaism. It was a common rabbinical term in Jesus' day, refering to what was either allowed or forbidden in temple services. Stern says that Christian binding, based on the rabbinical context of the word, is the *rule* of the church being exercised on earth. In other words, where the reign of our God and king is in place, the powers of darkness are bound. Where our God is not yet in charge, darkness prevails and needs to be bound.

A working definition of binding I find helpful is *to choke off darkness in order that God's light can shine into souls*. When Jesus confronted evil, he didn't argue, plead, or negotiate. He didn't use the word *bind* to win arguments. He took charge and issued commands to the powers of darkness by his Father's authority.

"I'M GOING TO KILL YOU!"

One young mother learned about choking off the power of darkness one night on a trip to the grocery store. She was apprehended at gunpoint as she stepped into her car at a grocery store parking lot. The man carrying the gun said, "Get in the car and drive! I'm going to rape you, and then kill you."

This woman shot a quick desperation prayer to the Lord. "O God, O God, O God!" The thought came to her, "Don't fall apart. Instead, look him in the eye and show him the love of God."

She said, "You're not going to kill me. You are going to allow God to touch your heart and heal you with his love. To be as upset as you are, you must have experienced a lot of pain in life." Her words stunned him. She continued, explaining the love of God in a compelling way. Two hours later she had gained his trust and convinced this escaped convict to turn himself in to the police. He did so without incident. Later when the local newspapers asked how she defended herself she simply said, "Instead of fighting him, I asked God to fill me with his love. I think God melted that man's heart and changed everything."

EVADE, PERVADE, INVADE

Christians take a number of approaches as they attempt to deal with darkness. Some try to bind darkness with an *evade* approach; that is, binding evil with the power of holiness. Evaders speak about the need to "come apart" from the world (see 2 Corinthians 6:17). By removing themselves from the world in as many ways as possible, they feel protected from evil and believe darkness has been dealt with adequately. Evaders are accurate in recognizing that we live in a world beset by darkness, but their desire to flee, while it can appear to honor God, is often based on fear. The underlying attitude of those who seek to evade darkness is "out of sight, out of mind."

The Apostle Paul makes it clear he was not an evader when he said, "I have written you not to associate with sexually immoral people—not at all meaning the people of this world who are immoral…. In that case you would have to leave this world" (1 Cor 5:9b, 10b). Despite their good intentions, evaders are hiding from darkness, not changing it.

EVADE

Other Christians try to bind darkness by *pervading* it; that is, overtaking it through the power of confrontation in the political, organizational, or spiritual realm. If the evader's motto is *Run Away!*, the pervader's rally cry is *Run 'em Over!*

While it is sometimes appropriate for Christians to be politically active, when we take our actions to an extreme we can look more political than Christian. The underlying attitude is, "We're big, we're bad, and we're taking over this city!" The more organized we become politically, the weaker our most powerful weapon—love—becomes.

There's no question that we must be active in the world, but what is the best strategy? I believe it's jumping in head-first, armed with the practical love of God.

PERVADE

Scripture and common sense tell us there is a time to flee from evil. There is also a time to fight evil head-on. Both the evasion and pervasion approaches to dealing with darkness have a measure of effectiveness, but both are dangerously close to an attitude that is antithetical to the spirit of Christ. There is a "we're right and you're wrong; we're in and you're out" smugness in both of these approaches. Rather than expressing the healing love and gentleness of Christ, we can develop outright disdain for the world that Jesus loved enough to die for.

When Jesus confronted darkness he didn't use evasion or pervasion. Rather, he *invaded* it with his own light. In servant warfare we invade darkness with light. We operate on the assumption that "greater is he who is in you than he who is in the world." Because he was convinced of the power of God, Jesus was in the world, but not of the world. He loved the world, but the love of the world was not in him. He desires the same paradoxical love to be in us.

When darkness and light cross paths, conflict is inevitable. God wants us to learn what it takes to effectively bind the strong man so that when we encounter darkness, we can render it ineffective and set free those who have been slaves to its power.

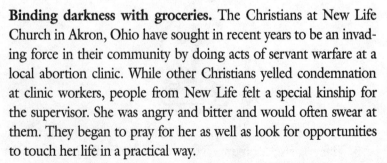

INVADE

Binding darkness with groceries. The Christians at New Life Church in Akron, Ohio have sought in recent years to be an invading force in their community by doing acts of servant warfare at a local abortion clinic. While other Christians yelled condemnation at clinic workers, people from New Life felt a special kinship for the supervisor. She was angry and bitter and would often swear at them. They began to pray for her as well as look for opportunities to touch her life in a practical way.

They discovered she was a single mom with several teens at home. The following Saturday morning they filled the back seat of her car with groceries. She cried in response to their kindness, and it wasn't long before she was asking them to pray for her. Though she hasn't yet come to Christ, she now calls her Christian friends regularly to request prayer.

If we hope to approximate the lifestyle of Jesus we must leave the safe confines of a Christians-only world. To avoid building a Christian ghetto we must invade the world with the love of God.

JESUS CHRIST: BINDER OF DARKNESS

The goal of all binding, as Jesus modeled it, is to liberate lives trapped in darkness so they might commit themselves more fully to God. Jesus "prohibited" darkness wherever he found it.

Jesus had many options available to him for battling darkness. Angels were at his disposal. Because the power of God rested upon him, he could have called upon the Lord like Elijah did on Mt. Carmel and wiped out his enemies in one fell swoop (see 1 Kings 18). On occasion Jesus did move in miraculous power, but he preferred to use a variety of tools to usher in his kingdom: miraculous works, inspired words, and works of practical mercy.

It's exciting to watch a gifted person speak eloquent words or even perform miracles, but most Christians can't picture themselves using these weapons for spiritual warfare. On occasion an unusual baseball player comes along who is ambidextrous; that is, he can bat either left-handed or right-handed. While it may be hard to picture Jesus playing baseball, I believe he was ambidextrous in the way he advanced his kingdom. He moved from person to person, approaching each one according to the need at hand. In his right hand he wielded the power of kindness while in his left he swung the power of miracles. Jesus declared war on human brokenness when he stated early in his ministry the reason he came to earth: He has sent me to proclaim freedom for the prisoners (see Luke 4:19).

This freedom came as he bound darkness using the power of miracles, such as:

- driving out demons (see Luke 4:31-41)
- praying for healing (see Luke 5:12-26; John 5:1-15)
- raising the dead (see Luke 7:11-17)
- miracles of nature (see Luke 8:22-25).

In other cases Jesus powerfully and authoritatively ordered away a demonic presence, usually with a single-word command. The most common word Jesus used in these meetings with evil was *ekballein*, which means to *cut off*, to *choke*, to *drive away*.

During one of Jesus' first sermons a demon appeared as he spoke to a hometown crowd (see Luke 4:31-37). When this spirit tried to disrupt him Jesus gave a short command: "Be quiet!" The demon left abruptly and the onlookers were amazed. They were startled because Jesus operated with such power.

In Matthew 17:18 Jesus rebuked a demon that was plaguing a little boy. In Luke 4:39 Jesus again rebuked a fever that was apparently caused by a demonic spirit, and it left Peter's mother-in-law. Most of the gospel accounts demonstrate that when Jesus crossed the path of a demonic power, it cried out for mercy.

Jesus also bound darkness in a variety of less dramatic but equally powerful ways, such as:

- washing the feet of the apostles (see John 13:1-17)
- teaching the truth of God (see Matthew 5, 6, 7)
- caring for the poor (imprisoned, hungry, naked, thirsty) (see Matthew 25:31-46).

Jesus was skilled at multiple approaches to war. Whether he used hand-to-hand combat or practical kindness, Jesus bound darkness as he encountered it and brought light where darkness had reigned.

LEARNING TO USE BOTH HANDS

Over the past couple of decades evangelicals have become more interested in combining practical ministry with moving in the power of the Holy Spirit. Peter Wagner coined the term *third wave* to describe this movement of the Spirit among evangelicals.[2] Conservative evangelicals and many others in the body of Christ have awakened to an undeniable reality: We must have the power of the Spirit resting upon us if we hope to make a difference in the world.

One evangelical writer I've particularly learned from is Charles Kraft, professor of anthropology and intercultural communication at Fuller Seminary, School of World Mission. Kraft points out that most people in the world must *feel* something before they are convinced to believe in it. This need for experience in order to trust things of the spirit is especially true outside Western culture. In an article, the professor points out that conversion occurs as a series of encounters beginning with a *power encounter*, then a *truth encounter*, and finally a *commitment encounter*.[3]

◆◆◆

Conversion occurs as a series of encounters.

◆◆◆

When third-wavers speak of a power encounter, they are referring to the dramatic meeting of darkness and light. A power encounter could be a healing, miraculous knowledge (a "word of knowledge," as Paul calls it in 1 Corinthians 12:8), or the casting out of a demon. God often uses a power encounter to get people's attention and shake loose satanic forces from the lives of those we seek to bring to Christ.

The truth encounter is the effective presentation of the gospel message so that non-Christians can deeply comprehend our words. The commitment encounter is bringing them into relationship with Christ through prayer.

I often hear Christians ask, "Why isn't revival happening here like it is in other parts of the world?" That question has been asked hundreds of times over the past few years by Christians who have read about significant moves of God around the globe. The implication behind the question is that what is going on *there* ought to be going on *here,* and if we become more committed, it will.

Be careful not to cause spiritual whiplash. A zealous pastor friend of mine who has read about the works of God "over there" became so fired up recently he said, "My goal is to see visitors to our church have a power encounter on their first visit that is so strong they'll either be drawn to Christ and join our church, or they'll not dare come back a second time." I appreciate his enthusiasm, but I find his attitude naive. He might build a church that may work well in South America, but won't go over in middle America.

◆◆◆

American culture does not comprehend
dynamic spiritual power.

◆◆◆

That pastor is overlooking a vital point: American culture does not comprehend dynamic spiritual power. One reason the kind of revivals that happen in the Third World don't often occur here is that if they did, Americans wouldn't get it! Compared to most people in the world, we have a relatively narrow view of the spiritual realm. Most cultures assume the existence of an active spirit world, but ours doesn't. Our culture treats the supernatural like it might exist, but assumes it can't be understood. Manifestations of power don't usually "compute" here.

In the early years of planting a church in Cincinnati, I saw many non-Christians dramatically touched by the power of God, yet not a single one ever joined the church. In our first years as a congregation we held ministry times at the close of our services during which we allowed those who believed they had a word of knowledge, prophecy, or wisdom to share before the group.

Once a young man had a word of knowledge that someone was present who was planning to rob a bank the next day. My first reaction to that was, "This person is kooky! There's no way a bank robber is here among us." A few minutes later an ashen-looking man came forward for prayer. To my chagrin, he admitted he had indeed been planning to rob a bank, and he wanted to repent!

I left church that day full of excitement. I thought, "All right! Finally the power of God is showing up here. No doubt, we're on our way to big things. We're going to see this guy converted and he'll bring his friends and family." But that guy never came back.

Later I had another power encounter, but this time in a college classroom. I was invited to speak to a philosophy class studying existentialism. They wanted to discuss the existence of God. After talking for the better part of the hour and getting nowhere, I concluded by saying, "We could argue for the rest of this semester. Let's pray and ask God to show himself to us, if he is real." As we sat quietly, I saw in my mind's eye a young guy keeled over holding his stomach. I felt the pain was like a muscle spasm in the abdominal area. With timid boldness I shared my picture and asked if anyone present needed healing in that way. Most of the students rolled their eyes as though to say, "You've got to be kidding!" but that all changed as soon as a young guy raised his hand and admitted I had described his condition to a "T." As I invited the Holy Spirit to heal his stomach, that young man was dramatically healed. After a few minutes he asked, "What do I do now?" I suggested he might want to give his life to the God who had just healed him — and he did just that! He received Christ right on the spot but never visited our church.

When we use power encounters with non-Christians in Western culture, we often give them spiritual whiplash. Secular Westerners aren't conditioned to take the jolt involved in a power encounter. In spite of our curiosity about the spirit world, Westerners are afraid of the dark. Western culture has a postcard-sized frame of reference regarding spiritual reality while most of the rest of the world sees it through a poster-sized frame. When a Westerner encounters dramatic spiritual power, the experience usually goes off the frame. What *convinces* in the Third World, *confounds* in the Western world.

I agree with Professor Kraft's assessment that we need to involve non-Christians in power encounters even in Western cultures, but we need to define power a bit differently. We must differentiate between a *soft* versus a *sharp* power encounter. A *soft* power encounter, emphasizing practical love, kindness, and mercy, will be more readily received and understood here than will a *hard*, dramatic display.

Fine-tune your use of soft power. If we hope to bind darkness in our culture, we need to become fluent in the use of soft power encounters. We need sharp power encounters to be a part of our arsenal, but we must face the fact that our culture doesn't recognize or value the spirit world. If we won't win any battles without God's might, and power encounters don't register on small spiritual frames, where does that leave us? In the words of Paul, we must "overcome evil with *good*" (Rom 12:21). Servant warfare is a subtle type of power encounter, and in the Western world today, it is often the most appropriate way to bind darkness. By demonstrating kindness in the power of the Holy Spirit, we will enlarge people's spiritual borders.

Serving as a means to bind darkness is nothing new. The church has followed this model since its beginning. The first formal appointment of leadership of the church in Jerusalem was assignment of deacons (see Acts 5). Traditionally the church has viewed the choosing of deacons as simply a practical move intended to free up time for the apostles to attend to more important leadership roles. While it's clear the deacons played a practical role in the early church, they served far beyond this by binding darkness through acts of service.

◆◆◆

If we hope to bind darkness in our culture, we need to become fluent in the use of soft power encounters.

◆◆◆

Internal fighting had begun in Jerusalem when the Jewish widows received more care than their Gentile counterparts. The apostles installed deacons, or *diakonos*, who by their Greek definition literally *waited on tables*. To view their serving as only practical is to miss a larger spiritual truth. As these deacons served the people in practical ways, they bound darkness. The plan worked, the church thrived, and instead of being known for their discord, observers of the early Christians exclaimed, "See how they love one another!"

Remember, as we do small things with great love we will change the world. *The Wizard of Oz* again provides an illustration of this principle. A small deed by Dorothy bound darkness, changed and liberated her friends. She had no idea how profound a difference she would make when she stepped forward to put out the flames on the Scarecrow with a bucket of water. She wasn't a very good shot, and water spilled over onto the Wicked Witch of the West. What she and her friends had desperately sought to do throughout their journey was accomplished with a simple bucket of water. The witch was destroyed.

But then that's Hollywood—and the kingdom of God as well.

Pair and Share Questions

1. How have you viewed the word "binding" in the past? As prayer? Words? Actions?

2. Define binding as you now understand it.

3. Using the evade, pervade, invade imagery, determine in which model you would place yourself and your church. Discuss anything you would like to do differently in the future.

4. Binding can be done "with a cannon or a slingshot." Give examples of each from your experience.

5. Professor Kraft describes the power encounter, truth encounter, and commitment encounter. Briefly share the story of your conversion in light of this model.

6. Have you personally experienced a "sharp power encounter"? What was your reaction?

7. Have you personally experienced a "soft power encounter"? What was your reaction?

8. Which power encounters, sharp or soft, had a more life-changing, lasting effect on you?

9. In what specific ways could you begin to bind the powers of darkness in your world?

RENOVATING MINDS

We do not remember days, we remember moments.
— Cesare Pavese —

Mickey Mantle was my childhood baseball hero. Mantle lived for years with the assumption that he probably wouldn't live past forty since none of the males in his family had survived beyond that age. Though he lived long past forty, he developed a "why fight it?" mentality, and lived as hard as he played ball. Though his baseball skill earned him a place in the Hall of Fame, alcoholism destroyed his gains, and ultimately led to his untimely death. Mantle's view of life had held him captive.

Jesus often used metaphors to teach people spiritual truths, and in Luke 11 he drew on a metaphor he was familiar with, carpentry, comparing the human mind to a house: "When an evil spirit comes out of a man, it goes through arid places seeking rest and does not find it. Then it says, 'I will return to the house I left'" (Lk 11:24).

This house to which Jesus was referring includes our emotions, opinions, and the way we view life—whether that view is true or false. When we have accurate views we live in freedom, but false views take us captive. Jesus said this house of the mind is sometimes held captive by a *strong man*, an obvious allusion to the enemy. For change and healing to occur, the strong man must be removed.

Jerry was a local musician who followed his own version of Hinduism. I was glad when his co-worker brought him to visit our church, but I was downright surprised when he continued to come regularly. He didn't agree with most of what I said in my sermons. He had an interesting way of showing his disapproval: He would shake his head vigorously from side to side—distracting to say the least!

◆◆◆

"God used both his Word and the love of
Christians week after week to change
my view and my heart."

◆◆◆

Over a period of eighteen months I noticed that Jerry was changing: His head shaking became less pronounced, and finally stopped completely. One Sunday he nodded his head "yes," indicating he wanted to receive Christ as Savior. Later, his friends exclaimed, "Boy, have you had a turnaround! What changed your mind about God?" He said, "I think God used both his Word and the love of Christians week after week to change my view and my heart."

There are many ways the strong man can be removed from the house of the mind. When Jesus cast a demon out of a man born deaf and mute in Luke 11, he was removing the strong man. Some Christians advocate Bible reading and prayer as the best way to bring liberation. But I have found over and over that simple kindness can be the most powerful means for entering houses of the mind that languish in darkness. Of the many valid ways to deal with the power of strongholds, the kindness of God seems to be the simplest way for everyday followers of Jesus to make a difference.

LOVING PEOPLE INTO THE KINGDOM

One Sunday morning in the early days of the Vineyard in Cincinnati, an energetic lady named Barbara rushed up to me with a panicked look on her face. "Do you know who that is?" she asked as she pointed toward a tall, middle-aged man. "That's Sam, a business owner who used to frequent the place where I was a bartender."

"Fantastic! I'm glad he's here."

That wasn't what Barbara hoped to hear.

She pulled her Bible out from under her arm and began to aim it at me. "But you don't know about him. He's an alcoholic. He's married, but unfaithful to his wife. It gives me the creeps that he's here. I don't think people like that should be allowed here."

"Well, what would you do with him if you had your way?" I asked Barbara.

"That's easy. I would confront him with his sin. I'd let him have it right between the eyes with the truth of God. He's a low-life and he needs to know that."

I was a little taken aback by Barbara's comments. After all, by her own admission, she was the bartender who had served Sam in the past! But after being a Christian for a few years, Barbara was less than graceful.

"Well, Barbara, I don't know him yet, but I'm pretty sure he already knows he's a sinner. Didn't you know you were a sinner before you came to Christ? I think we should treat Sam just like we treated you when you first came here. If we love him as he is, God will change him. Isn't that how you changed from being like Sam to being who you are today?" I could tell I had struck Barbara's heart. She quit aiming at me and began to cry.

That Sunday marked the beginning of an internal rebuilding project God has conducted in Sam and in Barb for several years. Sam and his wife joined a small group that poured large doses of kindness and mercy upon them. Within a couple of months the environment of love in that group convinced both of them to open their hearts and trust Christ. Sam's attitude changes showed up in obvious ways. Quietly his drinking came to a stop. He became faithful to his wife. He had learned to give and receive love from her. Though he'd never stepped into a church until he was nearly fifty, at fifty-two he was leading others to Christ and conducting a weekly Bible study.

Barbara has reflected deeply on who she used to be and is thankful for those who were patient with her. She has stopped defining people by their past, looking ahead to what they could become in Christ.

We all need to learn to look beneath the surface of people's lives to the deeper work God is doing. Change happens in most of us gradually, not through a sudden metamorphosis. Unfortunately, the power of kindness is often overlooked by a contemporary church that values the quick, even the instant transformation.

CONVERSION ISN'T BUILT IN A DAY

Imagine the church as a naval aircraft carrier cruising at high sea. All around the ship people are flailing in the dangerous waters. Suppose the crew had just one mission: to bring as many people as possible onto the safety of the deck. The goal for everyone in the water would be not only to get on board, but also to join the ranks and continue the outreach to the drowning. For this dramatic rescue to succeed, everyone would have to progress through the following steps: **Open Sea** —> **Lifeboat** —> **Sickbay** —> **Flight School** —> **Flight Deck.**

The people who need to be rescued are at the mercy of the *open sea* and its elements. The longer they stay in the water, the lower their chances for survival. In the world today millions are spiritually floating at sea, at a great distance from God.

Closer to the ship are the people in *lifeboats*. They have made their way out of the water, and are looking for the safety of the ship, but they don't know how to get there. Thousands of these "seekers" in the world today are looking for spiritual answers to life's problems. Every day some of these boat people find their way to the ship and are saved from the open sea.

Once on board, these survivors are shown to the *sick bay* where they're examined and healed from the ravages of the elements. Similarly, each new believer starts out in the "hospital" zone of the church.

Once on their feet, they are advanced to *flight school* where they discover their unique gifts and are equipped to rescue others outside the ship. Finally, they move to the *flight deck* where they contribute to the overall effort of bringing more and more people to safety.

BUILDING SPIRITUAL DWELLINGS THAT LAST

Paul made it clear that conversion to Christ is always a process when he said, "I planted, Apollos watered, but God gave the increase" (1 Cor 3:6). Jesus gave a similar paradigm for spreading God's love when he described the kingdom going forward like a sower scattering seed in a field. As the seeds were scattered, they fell on different soils. Jesus compared the soils to the different states of the human heart. The seeds grew in the various soils at different rates, and while most didn't bear fruit, some eventually produced an abundant harvest (see Matthew 13:1-30).

In the book, *What's Gone Wrong with the Harvest*[1], the process of conversion is illustrated by the Engel's Scale. Using this tool we can measure the spiritual "temperature" of a non-Christian from a minus ten to a minus one. If we hope to exert influence on our generation, we must recognize not only where individuals are on the Engel's Scale, but also how far our culture has strayed from the knowledge of God.

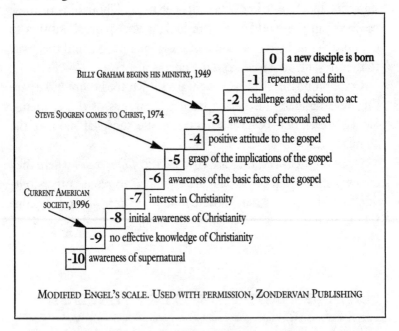

MODIFIED ENGEL'S SCALE. USED WITH PERMISSION, ZONDERVAN PUBLISHING

In *Conspiracy of Kindness,* I mentioned that Paul Benjamin's research in the mid-1970s showed that a typical non-Christian required five "significant encounters" before accepting Christ as Savior. My unscientific interviews with converts who received Christ during that time backs up Benjamin's conclusion. I would guess that if we could study converts from the late 1940s when our nation was at a minus four (positive attitude to the gospel), we'd discover that only three or four significant encounters were needed prior to conversion. In other words, as our culture moves further into the minus scale, a larger number of significant encounters is necessary to catalyze conversion.

Author and professor Dr. George Hunter gave words to my hunch in a recent conversation when he conjectured that the average convert to Christ today will require between twelve and twenty "significant touches" before they are saved. He added, "That means you'll be cleaning a lot of toilets in the years to come!"

It isn't just salvation that's a process; Christian growth takes place slowly as well. Once we come to Christ we all need to circulate from the sick bay to the flight school to the flight deck. Serving on the flight deck often incurs injury, so a return to the sick bay is not uncommon. Periodically we also need a stint in the flight school to upgrade our ministry skills.

◆◆◆

The average convert to Christ today will require between twelve and twenty "significant touches" before they are saved. That means you'll be cleaning a lot of toilets in the years to come!

◆◆◆

We must understand that it takes time to move from the sick bay to flight school to the flight deck. I'm concerned that if we're impatient with non-Christians and new Christians, we will damage instead of restore them.

BLUEPRINT FOR TRANSFORMING LIVES

Lovingkindness is the tool God uses to renovate the minds of non-Christians. This particular quality of God's draws each of us to him. The Hebrew word *hesed* refers to God's mercy and faithfulness. As Jeremiah puts it, "I have drawn you with lovingkindness" (31:3). The New Testament calls this same characteristic the "kindness of God" (Rom 2:4). It was this power that drew the prodigal son back to his father (see Luke 15).

Patient-kindness not only changes those we serve, but the Holy Spirit changes *us* as we walk in that attitude.

◆◆◆

Though I had been a Christian for years, it never
occurred to me that how I treat all others—not
just those above me—mattered to God.

◆◆◆

When the wife of a prominent East Asian manufacturer attended a serving seminar recently in the US, she was at first miffed at some of what I taught. The idea of serving others who are less advanced socially or educationally was offensive to her Indian culture. In that context, serving is noble only when it is aimed at those who are "equal" or "above" on the life accomplishment ladder. When she returned home, the idea of serving the poor began to grow on her, so she went down to the local community center to volunteer for whatever task they assigned her. Her job: bathing and caring for adult retarded folks. At first, when her husband and her pastor saw her radical behavior, they thought she might be having some kind of emotional breakdown!

After some months of living in the power of patient-kindness, I found her reflective thoughts touching: "Even though I had been a Christian for years, it never occurred to me that how I treat all others—not just those above me—mattered to God. I'm changing. I'm becoming a generous person. *I'm beginning to see others through the eyes of God!*"

We mirror to the world the life of God as we extend patient-kindness. This tool may not accomplish change quickly, and sometimes it's hard work to serve others. But kindness flowing through you and me in the power of the Holy Spirit will penetrate darkened minds and rebuild them on a new foundation.

Pair and Share Questions

1. How has your spiritual journey resembled the renovation of a house? What stage of the process are you in?

2. Can you identify specific areas in which God is changing your mind and heart?

3. In what sector of the aircraft carrier model do you find yourself? Explain your answer.

4. Do you see value in spending time in the sick bay? flight school? Why or why not?

5. "We mirror to the world the life of God as we extend patient-kindness." Discuss the implications of this statement to your Christian life today.

6. Using Appendix One, determine together a project your group could sponsor that would allow your kindness to bump up people in your community on the Engel's Scale.

8

LOVING OUR NEIGHBORS TO FREEDOM

When you get right down to the root
of the meaning of the word "succeed,"
you find it simply means to follow through.
— F. W. Nichol —

Sometimes in our desire to be useful to God we overlook the obvious. We pray, study, and give to further God's kingdom, but we don't meet the opportunities on our own doorstep. Our neighbors, co-workers, and our own families are the people we care the most about, but often they are the most difficult to attract to the Christian life. The good news is that the weapon of kindness is powerful enough to bring about change even in this spiritually challenging group.

When we lived in California, not long after we moved into our first house, my wife Janie and I picked up on the tension between a couple of our neighbors. One was a very outspoken churchgoer, while the other was an unbeliever. I knew I was in the hot seat when the unchurched man struck up a conversation with me as we were both working in our yards.

"Say, Steve, aren't you a pastor?" It seems implicit in the public's understanding that pastors exist to serve as referees in times of conflict, so I reluctantly listened as this troubled man opened up about the neighbor he'd never understood. He unfolded a long history of numerous conflicts over small issues.

"On occasion he and his family do a *drive-by shaming* of us." I asked what he meant. "You know, when they try to make us feel bad because we aren't like them." Then he looked up and sighed, "But the most recent problem takes the cake. We received a letter from his attorney threatening to sue us if we don't trim a tree that borders his yard. It seems strange he didn't just come over and ask me to take care of the tree before he went to his attorney."

As he told this story I reflected on earlier meetings I'd had with this Christian neighbor. When he heard I was a pastor he enthusiastically shared, "We're committed to fulfilling the Great Commission. We go door-to-door. You know, whatever it takes to win souls." I told him about the servant projects we do. "I'm committed to winning others to Christ, too," I said, "but these days I'm taking more of a *Flipper* approach to winning others by serving my way into their lives. I've found that a bad day with Flipper is better than a good day with Jaws." I could tell by the look on his face that he didn't understand the language of kindness I was trying to explain. All he could say was, "Uh, yeah, whatever."

As I listened to my distraught neighbor, I wished I'd been a better instructor in the ways of kindness. With a little wink this streetwise unchurched man continued, "You know, I was getting ready to trim that tree until this letter arrived, but now there's no way I'm going to do anything until he forces me. I will gladly go to court just so I can have a story to tell about being sued by Christians over an orange tree." He summarized his thoughts with a haunting observation: "I guess sometimes Christians love us—they just don't *like* us."

Ironically, my conservative Christian neighbors faithfully attended a church that is well-known for its emphasis on outreach. No doubt they had heard many messages about how to treat others, yet every week they'd pull into their driveway after church and live the rest of the week in opposition to the attitude of Christ.

◆◆◆

*I guess sometimes Christians love us—
they just don't like us.*

◆◆◆

Jesus' simple charge to us, "Love your neighbor as yourself," is not one to take lightly. Michael Hart, author of *The 100*,[1] has also observed that the element most often missing throughout the history of the church is practical love. His book ranks the top 100 most influential figures in history. I thought it odd that Jesus came in at number three, after Mohammed and Sir Isaac Newton. Hart apologizes for this inferior placement, adding that if the ranking system placed historical figures on their own merits alone, Jesus would hold the number-one spot hands down. Hart places Jesus third because of the poor job his followers have done over the centuries in carrying out their Savior's teachings. "Jesus' most distinctive teaching, (i.e., 'love thy neighbor')…," writes Hart, "remains an intriguing but basically untried suggestion."[2]

It's difficult to explain the discrepancy between the words and works of the founder of Christianity and those of his followers. My neighbors, like many Christians, were certainly aware of Christ's command to love their neighbor, but they seemed oblivious to the opportunity to love that Jesus placed literally in their own backyard. First, they needed to *recognize* their neighbor for who he was: a person Jesus told them to love. Second, they needed to realize that loving one's neighbor is *critical* to furthering the kingdom.

WHO IS MY NEIGHBOR?

A sarcastic lawyer once asked Jesus, "Who is my neighbor?" Jesus gave an in-depth answer in the form of the Good Samaritan parable (see Luke 10:25-37). When Jesus told the Good Samaritan story, he spoke to people who were no less fearful and suspicious than we are in our culture today. Theirs was a time of violence. It might well have been someone in their day who coined the phrase, "Good fences make for good neighbors." Yet Jesus didn't let them off the hook. He lionized the last person his audience expected: a lowly Samaritan who moved beyond his fears and helped a stranger in need.

The Samaritan showed authentic love for his neighbor in three ways. First, he was *practical*. He didn't just notice the man's plight, but he stepped out to bring relief, even when giving that was costly. Second, he was *patient* in his love. Even though there was no indication that the wounded man believed in the Lord, the Samaritan believed his kindness was a worthwhile investment that would pay spiritual dividends eventually. Finally, the Samaritan loved with *perception*. He saw more than a bleeding man; he recognized that the man lying at his feet was an assignment from God.

◆◆◆

Our most obvious neighbor is literally
the person next door.

◆◆◆

I have found that our neighbors usually come in one of three packages. Our most obvious neighbor is literally the *person next door*. Whether you recognize it or not, God has assigned you to the neighborhood in which you live. God strategically arranges our lives so we might be carriers of his life into the world. As you look at your living arrangements, have you seen them through the lens of God's assignment for you?

A friend told me recently that though he could afford a larger and more expensive house, after prayer and discussion he and his wife have decided to stay in their present home because they sense fruitful ministry opportunities are around the corner. If God really does place us in our neighborhoods, then our role shifts from being mere inhabitants to being infiltrators assigned to share the love of Christ.

◆◆◆

Our neighbor is the next needy person
God brings across our path to love.

◆◆◆

Our neighbor may also be the *person at the next desk*. Perhaps you haven't seen your vocational position as an assignment from God, but how would your view of work change if you recognized that he strategically placed you in your job so you could further his kingdom?

For many of us, the most challenging neighbor will be the *person with the toothbrush next to ours*. The most taxing spiritual warfare is waged for those under our own roof. It's great to be used by God to win the world, but a far greater challenge is setting out to win the people closest to us. When we look at it that way, the Great Commission may seem more like the Great Mission Impossible!

In short, our neighbor is *the next needy person God brings across our path to love.*

"BUT YOU DON'T KNOW *MY* NEIGHBOR!"

There's a lot of talk today about the necessity of setting boundaries to avoid living in codependency, but it can be a short step from establishing healthy limits to ordering our lives in such a way that God himself is prevented from giving us an assignment.

The reaction of many listening to Jesus tell that parable was probably a sarcastic, "Right. I'm sure." Or maybe they said it outright: "What are you talking about? No one can love like that except God himself!" To that Jesus would have said, "You're beginning to catch on!" He wasn't calling the world to try really hard to be nice, or to be more committed. He was inviting us to love with the very love of God himself.

Although I tend to be more task-focused than people-focused, I have been learning a bit lately about the kind of love Jesus talked about. Recently I was mowing my lawn when I ran across a number of huge dog piles. A few months ago we bought a small dog for our kids. Ever since then our neighbor's enormous dog has felt compelled to use our yard as a toilet to prove his dominance.

Encountering the giant dog piles made me more than a little irritated. I got angry and thought to myself, "I'm going next door now to set this thing straight. I've had it with cleaning up their doggie messes." On my way across the lawn I felt the Lord speak to me. "If you complain to your neighbors you'll get in the way of what I'm doing inside them. Instead, why don't you clean up the dog piles in their yard first, and then yours!"

As I make my clean-up rounds, I'm not sure anyone is changing besides me, but I'm confident that as I demonstrate the practical love of the Samaritan my neighbors will receive the love of Christ.

WHY IS IT DIFFICULT TO
LOVE THOSE CLOSEST TO US?

It is the love of God moving through us that changes the world, yet loving those we're most involved with can be difficult for a number of reasons.

Familiarity. The more we know others, sometimes the harder it is to love them. We seem to exhaust patience with those we've been with the longest. Last week at a restaurant I couldn't help but notice two couples sitting at nearby tables. One couple was apparently new in their relationship because they hadn't broken eye contact. She was convinced he was brilliant. He laughed at her every comment. The other couple had probably been married for years: They ate an entire dinner without even looking into each other's eyes. It looked like they'd heard and seen it all with each other.

Fear of disappointment. Let's face it, when we seek to bring someone to Christ one of two things happens: (a) they come to Christ, or (b) they don't. This simple proposition makes disappointment a big possibility. It's hard to pray and work toward bringing someone we love to Christ because we have so much invested emotionally. Sometimes it's easier to let someone else have faith for those we love the most.

Slow pace of change. I have found there is nothing slower than the process of loving our neighbors to Christ. But sometimes we give up too soon and pull out before God is able to finish his work. To become more patient in waiting for the harvest, we need a clearer picture of what it means to bear fruit.

GREEN, BRUISED, OR RIPE?

On the night of his arrest, Jesus issued a lifelong challenge to the apostles: "Go and bear fruit—fruit that will last" (Jn 15:16). There are many kinds of fruit Jesus might have had in mind that night in the Upper Room, but considering that this was his last night on earth, I believe he was referring to the ultimate fruit of human souls.

Millions of plants bear fruit, but regardless of the genus, all fruit appears in just three states: green, bruised, or ripe. Green fruit isn't ready for harvest. Bruised or damaged fruit needs special care if it's to be nourishing by harvest time. The goal is to produce ripe, luscious fruit that is ready to be picked. To reach this goal, the wise farmer approaches each kind of fruit with the appropriate strategy. From a spiritual perspective all of humanity is also either green, bruised, or ripe. Christians must learn the appropriate strategies for readying each kind for harvest.

Green fruit: Learning the language of love. All of us start out spiritually "green." Gradual seasoning is required to help those around us become spiritually ripe.

As a foreign exchange student in the 1970s I was immersed for a year in the Norwegian culture and language. Armed with only a few words, I began living with a Norwegian family and learned their language by the sink-or-swim approach. Similarly, God has a crash course in language acquisition in mind for the world. He desperately wants those outside of Christ to learn the language of love. His plan is to use Christians as tutors to provide the needed instruction. If unbelievers are to get to know God, we must be in close contact and constant interaction with them.

Losing old stereotypes. Everything I heard sounded like gibberish my first few weeks in Norway. I had seen the Swedish chef on *The Muppet Show,* and had that image in mind when I heard Norwegian being spoken. For a couple of months everyone spoke with the sing-song voice of that cook, and I had to resist the urge to laugh each time I heard the language spoken. At first, because I was an outsider, I felt like I was living among an entire population of Muppets.

Before I could make progress in learning the language, I had to get past the images I brought with me. This is also true in the spiritual life. Non-Christians must unlearn an old language they have spoken since birth. Jesus commented on this worldly mother tongue when he said, "When he [Satan] lies, he speaks his native language, for he is a liar and the father of lies" (Jn 8:44). Apart from Christ the only language we know is the dark language of the enemy that discolors God, life, and ourselves.

Those near us must first experience the language of love up close if they are to find God. As language tutors our first task is to help them unlearn inaccurate spiritual conclusions that are keeping them away from Christ. Once their skewed view of what a Christian is is altered, we can help them rebuild an accurate picture.

A traditional approach to battling for those in darkness is to pepper them with Scripture verses. If we throw too much information at them, however, they will not only get confused, but tragically their preconceived assumptions will also be reinforced. What they will hear is:

"I will love you *if* you believe like I believe."

"I will love you *if* you live like I live."

"I will love you *if* you behave properly."

In a world that offers conditional love, non-Christians listen for the "ifs." Most of us have witnessed to someone and had them interrupt us with the comment, "Before you say any more to me about God, I've got to tell you I'm trying about as hard as I can to be a good person." Non-Christians think that the goal of believers is to get them to behave rather than to trust Jesus by faith. Misconceptions die slowly. As our neighbors are conditioned to hear the language of love, their minds are slowly changed so that when we speak the words of God with love, their hearts respond.

Our unconditional serving will go a long way toward correcting caricatures and escorting our neighbors out of darkness. I am in regular contact with a home-group leader in Northern England who feels particularly called to reach out to the pub community in his city. For months his group members found it difficult to get past the deep-seated misconceptions pub-goers held about Christians, but when they began to serve their way into the pub, things changed. The British go to pubs not only to drink beer, but also to eat *crisps*, or potato chips, as they drink. This group has seen a complete turnaround in their outreach as they've handed out free crisps with a little card that explains, "We want to show you the love of Christ in a practical, salty way."

The group leader told me recently that many of those served have been stunned by this practical outreach. A light goes on in the hearts of those pub-goers with each bag of crisps and the conversations that often follow.

Becoming fluent. After a couple of months of constantly hearing Norwegian I began to recognize about every third word spoken around me. I was able to get the gist of what was spoken to me although I wasn't able to speak very well myself. After hearing a word ten or twenty times, I'd have an *ah-ha* experience.

After six months I had learned enough words and phrases to get by with my new language, but I wasn't fluent. As I compared notes with other exchange students, I found out that many got to this point and assumed they knew the language, when actually they sounded like Americans trying to imitate Norwegians. One American Christian friend thought he knew what he was doing when he translated a chorus that contained the line, "Come, Holy Spirit" at a church service one night. In Norwegian the words *spirit* and *duck* sound almost identical. This friend couldn't figure out why none of the several hundred people present wanted to join in with him as he taught them this new song. Norwegian etiquette doesn't allow for someone to actually correct another in public, so at the end of the evening an older lady approached my friend and said, "We think we know what you meant, but we just didn't feel right about singing, 'Come, holy duck.' It just didn't seem right!"

I knew I was getting becoming fluent in Norwegian when others would ask, "Where in Norway are you from?" I would still make an occasional grammatical mistake, but I could express myself in speech and writing with ease. I knew I was fluent when my host family asked me to close my bedroom door at night because I was keeping them awake by speaking Norwegian in my sleep!

◆◆◆

As we speak the language of love through serving, we break down the communi-cation barriers between the church and the world.

◆◆◆

The key to fluency is thinking in Norwegian. Once I began to think like Norwegians, I also began to talk like them. As we speak the language of love through serving, we break down the communication barriers between the church and the world. It may seem stiff to us at first, but a few faltering actions can eventually become a lifestyle of fluent kindness. Languages are learned the same way green fruit is ripened: *gradually.* If we are to be effective at leading captives out of darkness, we must value each change that takes place and rejoice in whatever progress is made.

Bruised fruit: Peter's prescription. Many of us have experienced the heartache of seeing someone we love resist our best efforts to bring them to Christ. It seems the most painful bruised fruits to deal with are those closest to us: resistant spouses, rebellious children, rejecting parents.

Mack was a recovering alcoholic who came to Christ during my first year of pastoring in Cincinnati. It wasn't long before one, then another of his adult children came to know the Lord until everyone in the family was committed to Christ, with one exception: Mack's wife Kathryn. Her continual comment to her children was, "I'm happy for you." For ten years Mack and his children watched her remain unmoved in spite of their best efforts. They tried everything they could think of to reach her: Bibles as gifts at Christmas, cassette tapes with convincing sermons, and even cornering her at family get-togethers. But nothing worked. Her daughter said, "In politically correct language, she is spiritually impaired!"

Fortunately the Bible gives us a strategy to use with the Kathryns in our lives. In the ancient world it was common for pagan women to follow in the spiritual footsteps of their husbands, but in early Christian circles that pattern didn't hold. The first-century church was distinguished by its high view of women. Luke's Gospel and the book of Acts make it clear that the early believers held women in high esteem, in contrast to the popular view of women as barely above the status of slaves. It was only natural that many women came to know Christ in the early church apart from their husbands' spiritual leadership.

In his first letter, Peter offered a simple strategy that worked for these frustrated women who wanted to see their husbands follow Christ.

> Wives, in the same way be submissive to your husbands so that, if any of them do not believe the word, **they may be won over without talk by the behavior of their wives,** when they see the purity and reverence of your lives... it should be that of your inner self, the unfading beauty of a **gentle and quiet spirit,** which is of great worth in God's sight.
>
> 1 Peter 3:1-4, emphasis mine

Perhaps you've assumed that Peter's counsel was meant only for women with unsaved husbands, but certainly that wasn't the apostle's intention. As in Mack's case, sometimes it's the wife who doesn't yet believe, or it may be a child or a parent. Commentator Peter H. Davids captures Peter's intention when he writes, "Peter's concern at this point is not life within the Christian community, but life at those points where the Christian community interfaces with the world around it."[3] Peter was empowering the entire church with a tool that any Christian can use when trying to bring bruised fruit to health. Peter's approach has four simple elements.

Love recklessly. The prevailing approach women had been taking was to argue their husbands into faith. Peter countered them, promising that "they may be won over without talk by... behavior" (v. 1). Peter's advice was to heap large doses of practical love upon unbelieving loved ones, not verbal debate. He calls believers to demonstrate a "gentle and quiet spirit." For years I thought Peter was calling women to mouse-like behavior, but that isn't accurate. Again, Peter H. Davids sheds light on Peter's intent: "'Gentle' in the Greek world was an amiable friendliness that contrasted with roughness, bad temper, or brusqueness.... 'Peaceful'... (was) the sense of being calm and tranquil as opposed to restless."[4] In other words, the best way to approach bruised people for Christ is through simple kindness. Peter wasn't calling women to tiptoe their way through life; he was urging all of us to abound in practical, peaceful friendliness.

Live consistently. Peter understood that some people will not believe as quickly as others and will require more time to come to a conclusion about Christ. He writes that they will come to faith "when they see your lives" (v. 2). Mack's wife, Kathryn, told me once when I asked why she was so resistant to following Christ, "I've never been one to jump on bandwagons. I'm a little resistant to become a Christian just because everyone else is going that direction." Peter understood that there is nothing like unwavering love to get the attention of unbelievers.

Arlo Guthrie, singer and songwriter of Woodstock fame, came to Christ a few years ago after searching out every corner of the spiritual world for decades. What sent him over the line toward Christ? He simply saw someone live out the love of God consistently. "I found somebody who loves God and is devoted to God as much as I think I want to be... her name is Ma.... This is somebody who, about five years ago, said, 'Come with me on my rounds.' I knew she was real because she did what Christ asked people to do: she fed the hungry, she clothed the naked, she comforted those in prison, she was jumping into bed with people with AIDS and hugging them while they died, and she was taking care of crack babies and AIDS babies. And she wasn't after any publicity. She wasn't offering any courses. There was nothing for sale."[5]

◆◆◆

"I found somebody who loves God and is devoted to God as much as I think I want to be."

◆◆◆

Jesus said that "the eye is the lamp of the body" (Mt 6:22). As the spiritually bruised see the life of God in us their hearts will be changed.

Listen Carefully. Once we've gotten someone's attention, it's only a matter of time before they start asking questions about spirituality. Through our actions, we show them we are different. Peter predicted they would naturally become curious and ask us about our relationship with God, so he advises us, "Always be prepared to give an answer to everyone who asks you to give the reason for the hope that you have. But do this with gentleness and respect...." (1 Pt 3:15).

In my dealings with the spiritually resistant, I've found they are more curious than they usually admit. Internal wheels are turning, even when we don't see any apparent progress. Peter says they will develop questions as they increasingly understand the language of love. Our role is to be available to give them an answer.

♦♦♦

*"When you give out groceries here, you
feed them for about a year."*

♦♦♦

There is a poor neighborhood in our city that I've brought groceries to for ten years. Often I have delivered food, prayed for folks, and gone my way without seeing much spiritual responsiveness, but I've continued to return year after year. On a recent trip a Christian resident commented, "When you give out groceries here, you feed them for about a year." I asked her to explain. "After you've been here, I and other believers are able to answer their questions and help them process the love they've been shown. Because you have helped to meet their physical needs by bringing food, they are very open to entering into a personal relationship with Jesus Christ. The openness lasts for about a year with each family you touch."

Wait patiently. In my early days as a Christian, I operated with the motto, "If they don't respond, increase the pressure." After strong-arming the spiritually resistant in my family, it became clear to me my approach wasn't helping any of them move toward Christ. Eventually I faced the fact that I'm limited in the change I can stimulate, and I turned to the only option possible: patience. Ultimately, after we have loved people, consistently lived among them with gentleness, and answered their questions, we must place them in the hands of God.

Peter's promise was that after we did all we could do, we would find rest as we "hope in God" (v. 5). I have seen many become frustrated at this point and single-handedly dismantle the work God is doing in their loved ones by doing one of two things: they stop caring, or they apply more pressure. Whatever your temptation might be, don't give up. Instead, pray. Patiently pay attention to what the Lord is doing in them, and thank God for his good work. Go back to loving them recklessly, being consistent, and answering their questions. If you can resist the desire to "corner" them, you'll find it's just a matter of time until they corner you.

◆◆◆

When we try to change hearts ourselves,
even though we have great motivation,
we simply get in the way of God's work.

◆◆◆

One of Kathryn's daughters came to me two weeks ago so excited she was literally jumping up and down. At first I thought she had won the Ohio Lottery! "I can't believe it," she bubbled. "My mom came to Christ last week!" I asked what she thought happened to change Kathryn after all these years. Her daughter put her finger on the key: "We quit bugging her! As we loved her and showed our appreciation for her, the Holy Spirit began to work directly upon her heart."

Our role in changing lives is to do the small stuff—loving, showing practical kindness, and being patient—as God does the big part of changing hearts. When we try to change hearts ourselves, even though we have great motivation, we simply get in the way of God's work. Some things change best when we stand back and let God be God.

Shortly before my family moved away from our litigation-prone Christian neighbors, we had another talk with them about God's heart for the neighborhood. My neighbor said, "You know, I've been thinking about what you said to me awhile back. I think it might work better to bring people out of darkness with a soft approach than a hard one." A week later, he and his family were going door to door, this time with tins of home-baked cookies in hand. **They've traded in drive-by shamings and legal threats for practical love.** I hear the neighborhood is changing.

Pair and Share Questions

1. What small things could you do to make a difference with your neighbors right now?

2. Do you know your neighbors well enough? or would God have you invest more time connecting with them?

3. Who are the "neighbors" God has placed in your life
   - next door?
   - at work?
   - at home?

4. How could you respond to the following situations to demonstrate God's love for your next-door neighbor?
   a. You live on a busy highway. Each morning you pick up the trash generated by the local fast-food restaurants. Your neighbor does not, and the garbage blows into your yard by the time you get home from work.
   b. You live in a well-manicured neighborhood. Your neighbor takes off for a three-week vacation and neglects to make arrangements for someone to mow his five-acre lawn.
   c. Your neighbor's two boys love to play baseball. The ball usually ends up in your garden.

5. As you look at your present living arrangements, have you seen them through the lens of God's assignment for you? If not, how would this insight change your behaviors?

6. How would your view of work and your co-workers change if you recognized that God specifically placed you in your job? How would that insight change your daily behavior?

7. Select a problem you're having or have had with a "neighbor"(someone in your neighborhood, workplace, or family). How could you have been more practical, patient, and perceptive in dealing with the situation?

8. Identify one individual in your life who is spiritually "green." How could you show this person "fluent kindness?"

9. Identify one individual in your life who is spiritually "bruised." How could you apply each element of Peter's prescription to help this person?

   a. love recklessly

   b. live consistently

   c. listen carefully

   d. wait patiently.

THE POWER OF SMALL GROUPS

The only true happiness comes from
squandering ourselves for a purpose.
— William Cowper —

I n the early days of planting the Vineyard in Cincinnati, the few
small groups we had were hungry for newcomers to join them,
so when Julie showed up one night she was received with open
arms by the other eight folks present. This single young woman
seemed normal enough at first, until after a leaf-raking outreach
one night she began to behave strangely.

Over a cup of coffee Julie confided, "You know, I'm very excited about what the Lord is doing in my life through this group. But
I know it can't last. You see, *they* aren't comfortable here." When
my wife asked what she meant by *they*, Julie said she had several
"spiritual guides" that were her inward companions. She said they
had been her secret friends for some years and helped her cope in
life. My wife pointed out that these voices might be demonic—
something Julie had suspected herself. Naturally, Janie offered to
pray to banish Julie's voices, but surprisingly, Julie was resistant. I'll
never forget her haunting, sad words: "They aren't much, but
they're all I've got."

No matter how much the group tried to convince her of their support, Julie resisted the offers of help; but she did continue to attend group meetings. Over the next few months she grew to trust these new friends. One night she finally opened up and asked for prayer. God's power was present, and Julie was set free.

WHY DO WARFARE IN SMALL GROUPS?

I find that Christians generally over-value weekend services and under-value small groups. We tend to view large gatherings the way many view the Bermuda Triangle: that place where unexplainable things happen. We see our services in an almost mystical way, assuming that if we could just get people to church on Sundays, something amazing would transpire inside them. Julie's transformation, however, came where the greatest changes usually take place: in groups of ten or fewer.

◆◆◆

*The popularity of small groups has
grown to an all-time high.*

◆◆◆

One doesn't have to look far in the New Testament to find that God works powerfully through small groups. In a sense, the Twelve that Jesus called to found the church functioned as a small group. Paul's letters make reference to groups meeting in homes, such as the one that met at Philemon's house (see Philemon 1:2).

Though small groups have been on-again, off-again in church history, for a number of reasons I believe they will prove to be one of the most effective tools at the disposal of the church in the coming years. Over the past decade America has become suddenly hungry for relationships that form naturally in small groups. In his book *Sharing the Journey*,[1] Robert Wuthnow reveals the statistic that the popularity of small groups has grown to an all-time high, with nearly 40 percent of the American adult population in a group of some sort. It seems only natural that God would use this potent setting as a tool for changing lives because groups provide so much of what hungry people are looking for.

Small groups provide relationship. Perhaps it has always been true that people are starving for relationship, but that seems to be an especially accurate hallmark of the present age. As workloads increase and leisure time shrinks, our culture will turn further away from traditional community. I believe small-group relationships will become increasingly welcomed as a way to counter people's isolated lifestyles.

Small groups model the Christian life. The world is unimpressed with words that aren't backed up by actions. Small groups can bring the message of God's love to their neighborhoods like no outsider can.

As a twist on our restroom cleaning outreaches, we had urinal screens for men's rooms imprinted with our church's logo and phone number. We reasoned, "We might as well leave a unique calling card once we've cleaned the bathroom!" I have been amazed at the number of letters I've received from men expressing their thanks for our service. One man's sentiments captured the response of many who've written: "I walked into the men's room at a restaurant and when I looked down, there was the Vineyard! This lowly service proved to me you guys are authentic."

As we serve in groups by cleaning bathrooms, raking leaves, washing windshields, or bringing food to needy families, we literally deliver the life of Jesus to our neighborhoods in unforgettable ways.

Small groups care. If your church has more than fifty members, your pastor is incapable of adequately meeting everyone's needs by himself. If church leaders hope to provide adequate care for Christians, we must either limit the size of our churches, or empower laypeople to take on the task of overseeing small groups that care for their members in regular, practical ways.

Small groups have courage. If it's true that less than 10 percent of Christians feel capable of doing spiritual warfare, then we need to find new ways of building courage into the body of Christ. Courage is often bolstered when responsibility is shared by a group. While leading a toilet-cleaning crew in Wichita, Kansas, we came across a biker bar called "The Shady Lady." I had started for the front door when my team said in unison, "We can't go in there. That's a biker bar!" I was up for the challenge but understood their reticence, so I agreed to clean this one by myself. Shortly after I entered, my timid team came in with sheepish looks on their faces. We had a great conversation with the owner while a number of the patrons listened intently. I'm convinced that God was able to do a larger work that day because of the courage our group found in being together.

Small groups have spiritual power. When even a few Christians gather, they present a powerful force of destruction to darkness. I've been leading a group of some sort continuously for almost twenty years, and I suspect I'll recommend groups for all the above reasons for the rest of my life, but I do have a concern. Part of the reason we join groups to begin with is to find healing for our brokenness. We all need healing. But I am convinced that in addition to looking inwardly, we also need to focus outwardly. As we give, we will be healed.

Continuous healing happens in our lives as we reach *out*, then reach *in*, and finally reach *up*. Before long, "reaching out" naturally becomes a "reaching in" exercise. As we are progressively healed of our wounds and hang-ups, we are more able to make sense of the perspective that comes as we reach up.

REACH OUT!

The first component of a healthy group is a commitment to helping others outside the group. As we stretch beyond ourselves we are healed.

◆◆◆

*I discovered that my groups had a fatal disease I wasn't aware even existed: **inward-itis!***

◆◆◆

After several years of leading small groups, I noticed it was consistently difficult to maintain a healthy group for more than a year. I couldn't figure out why. It didn't seem to matter where the group was located, the background of the members, or the maturity of the layleaders. After about twelve months, the group would dismantle itself from within. After years of watching this pattern I discovered that my groups had a fatal disease I wasn't aware even existed: *inward-itis!* An unchecked case of this virus becomes as deadly as an obstruction of the digestive system. Surprisingly, as soon as I added the element of regular outreach to my groups, they became healthier almost instantly and were able to extend their lifespans.

We are God's weapons against darkness. The question for a small group is not, "*Should* we reach out?" but "*Where* does God want us to focus our efforts?" God will answer that prayer before long by pointing out a specific assignment, such as a particular family or neighborhood to serve.

Several of our groups sense a particular burden for movie-goers around our city, so periodically they sponsor an ice cream cone giveaway to people going into theaters on Friday and Saturday nights. At a recent opening for an action movie, two small groups descended upon the several hundred people in line. The groups gave away coupons good for one cone at a local store. The reverse side of the coupon explained the point of the outreach.[2] The twenty group members gave away over 500 coupons and had many short bursts of conversation.

◆◆◆

The ice cream is nice, but I could use
some of your excitement.

◆◆◆

One person quizzed, "Why are you so fired up?" The young women giving away the coupons said, "We believe Jesus loves people enough to show it in a practical way." The startled woman answered, "The ice cream is nice, but I could use some of your excitement. You seem to actually enjoy life." They continued talking until the movie started.

We are servants. If Jesus said, "I did not come to be served, but to serve," how much more should that be true for his followers? Sometimes Christians forget that by definition we are "little Christs" going into the world with the identical intent of Jesus. Non-Christians have heard that it's better to give than to receive. They may not know who said it, or where it's found in the Bible, but they believe deep down that it's normal for Christians to serve.

If your group wants to make a difference, take an informal survey among your neighbors by asking, "What could I and my small group do to serve you in a practical way?" No doubt those you ask will be shocked at first! They probably won't have something to ask of you on the spot, but if you offer to come back in a few days they will have not only thought of something, but they may also say, "So, tell me about this Jesus stuff...."

We need to serve others to stay healthy. We must give of the life we've taken in or we'll stunt our spiritual growth. God designed us to flow with the life of God, as Jesus makes clear in the metaphor of the vine in John 15. There Jesus calls us branches. If you examine a cross section of a grape branch closely you'll see it resembles a straw, because that's how it functions. It receives life from the stock of the vine and allows the life force to pass through itself. Somehow, through no work of its own, the branch grows fruit at its end. We too must allow the life of God to pass through us if we are to produce healthy fruit.

Several of our men's groups have made a serving pact together. When heavy snows come and roads are closed, they take a partial day off, converge with snow blowers and shovels, and begin to dig others out of driveways. Last winter I spent half a day with a couple of these teams. The men made short work of the snow, clearing some walks and driveways in less than five minutes! I liked the sentiment of one guy: "If it's a bad snow day, I can't go to work as usual anyway. I like to redeem my time this way and have fun with my group at the same time."

We can make a profound impression. One of the reasons groups may resist outreach is that we think it's necessary to spend huge amounts of time preparing and carrying out our mission. Not so! It isn't the scale of an act of kindness that makes an impression, but the gesture. Even small acts of kindness can find their way deep into the memories of those who are spiritually darkened.

For example, do you remember a neighbor or relative who never forgot to send you a birthday card while you were growing up? I've met many people who've had an aunt or neighbor who remembered their birthday over the years, and this special person's simple faithfulness has made a deep impression. If you were to begin a birthday card campaign in your neighborhood, you might make a life-changing impression in the name of Christ.

Beyond seeing our role in new ways, we must build a specific and strategic small group serving plan. We don't always do what we *say* we value, we do what we *plan*. I recommend thinking along these lines:

Decide you are going to reach out. It's hard to find someone who doesn't believe outreach ought to be done, but just holding a value isn't enough. What is decided is what gets done.

Define a regular outreach schedule. Once you've said yes to outreach, schedule projects several months in advance. If your group meets weekly, do an outreach about once every four to six weeks. If your group meets every other week, do a project about every other month.

Try a simple, low-risk first project. Succeeding at something makes us want to try it again. Leaf raking, soft drink giveaways, or food delivery to single-parent families are all easy projects that are likely to give your group members a positive outreach experience. (Appendix 1 lists several servant warfare projects to consider. Also, more project ideas are found throughout my book, *Conspiracy of Kindness.*)

Celebrate your outreach successes. A down-loading time after your outreach is vital to help group members process their experience. Spend time together afterward over a cup of coffee, and swap stories and impressions of the experience. This will bring the group closer and build everyone's confidence for the next outing.

REACH IN!

Once we have sufficiently reached beyond ourselves, it's natural to reach inward. Several years after starting the Vineyard I had a significant conversation with a local Christian counselor. "People from your church make up about 50 percent of my counseling practice," he said. "I just called to thank you for starting your church here!"

His comments elicited questions from me. "You know, we have lots of small groups that are designed to bring healing to the wounded. Is what we're doing somehow wrong?"

"What's the ratio of healed to wounded in your groups?"

"It's more the other way around. We have about six broken people for every one healed."

"My perspective as a counselor is that a healthy group has about one broken person for every six healthy ones. I think I know why you have the exact opposite ratio. The outreach you do is great at bringing in the broken, but you have too many of them to deal with effectively."

My conversation with the counselor that day led me to an important discovery: Healthy groups that bring in a cross-section of people *create their own spiritual warfare*. The adage "I'm my own worst enemy" seems to hold true, unless groups can become effective at creating a genuinely healing atmosphere. Broken people need the love and mercy healed people have to offer. Likewise, the healed need the broken, for without a challenge to love with the love of God, they will not grow. So how do we wisely build an atmosphere for dealing with darkness for everyone involved?

Build a therapeutic atmosphere in your group. The job of small-group leaders is not to judge or categorize people by their past behavior, but to direct them to where they can most effectively be healed. Medical personnel use a *triage* approach to dealing with large numbers of wounded during battle. To save precious time, doctors sort the wounded by identifying them as superficially, moderately, or critically injured. As we successfully penetrate darkened lives through serving projects, those we touch will come to us with their emotional baggage. These new folks will need a small group setting in order to heal, but they'll need directing upon their arrival.

For years I made the mistake of failing to provide any sort of direction to new group members. As a result, the level of health in many of our groups was reduced to the lowest common denominator of the most unhealthy person present. Group leaders need to direct newcomers with particularly deep-seated issues to specialized groups so they can receive focused, appropriate care.

Establish a "first base." For many new Christians, the first step toward breaking free from their past is getting involved in a group that will help them identify their unhealthy ways of thinking. We've had great success by establishing a "first base" in the form of *Search Groups*. These groups are based on Robert McGee's insights in his book *Search for Significance*, an excellent treatment of the Twelve Steps from a biblical viewpoint.

Some people need to begin their walk in Christ with an examination of the way they relate to life. For many, discipleship may mean dealing with their personal recovery issues. Hundreds in my church have participated in a thirteen-week Search Group as a launching point, and then moved on to a long-term group. This strategy of establishing a starting point protects the long-term groups from unnecessary stress and quickly gets to the issues most new believers are dealing with.

Provide safety. We must offer help to hurting people, but how do we prevent them from dominating our groups? For years I resisted the practice of closing groups—that is, not allowing new members to join once a group got off the ground. I thought we'd create ghettos of the healed separated from the broken, but eventually I changed my mind as I watched the energy levels of group leaders drain as needy newcomers continually came into established groups. Now most of our long-term groups are open for three weeks when they begin, then closed to new members. This allows for a level of trust to be established and safe, healing relationships to form.

Equip group leaders. If we hope to empower layleaders to effectively deal with pastoral care tasks, we must expand their skills. With a few simple skills the average group leader can become effective at dealing with a multitude of issues that are commonly passed on to pastors. Laypeople can be trained to develop the following skills.

Listening. In our increasingly busy society it is rare for another human being to listen—to *really* listen. A businessman friend of mine has been particularly prolific at winning others to Christ by using a simple approach. He asks them, "How are you doing?" After they respond with an automatic "Fine," he responds back, "No, really, I mean it. How are you doing?" When they see he's open to really hearing from them, they often open their hearts. Sometimes he ends up praying for them. My friend makes an impression on others because as he listens he affirms their value.

◆◆◆

Listening is the most concrete expression
of grace to those in pain.

◆◆◆

We have all lived in a non-listening world long enough to crave having someone to really hear us. Valuing others is demonstrated, not verbalized. We show others they are genuinely valued as we listen to them with our full attention. Listening is the most concrete expression of grace to those in pain. Often hurting people will test our listening skills in order to judge the level of safety we're offering. Is what they shared treated with empathy and respect? If not, they don't dare go forward. Listening opens doors and proves our trustworthiness and authenticity.

Rational Christian thinking. The first several chapters of Acts describes how the Holy Spirit molded a community out of strangers. Not surprisingly, conflict arose when the Greek converts were being overlooked in the distribution of food, unlike their Aramaic-speaking counterparts. This conflict was resolved in part by someone simply listening and then offering objective feedback about the problem at hand (see Acts 6:1-7).

All of us have beliefs we've carried around for years as though they were true, even when they're false and damaging. These irrational, often unconscious ways of seeing reality cause daily problems for all of us. To get better we need to see the objective truth about life, not just the truth we have inherited from our families, or the truth of our own making. A caring, small-group context can be the ideal place for us to discover the lies we believe about life, relationships, God, and ourselves.

It's amazing how many of our beliefs about life don't make much sense once they're echoed back to us by a friend. Careful listening and rational feedback are powerful change agents that bring those stuck in dark ways of thinking into the light.

Speaking the truth in love. An excellent way to begin to speak the truth to hurting people is to serve as a sounding board by *clarifying* what we hear them saying. We can provide a valuable service when we point out apparent discrepancies and inconsistencies in what they share. Remember, our role is not to give commentary about the person, but rather to focus on the behavior he or she is struggling with. The goal in clarifying the truth is to love the sinner but hate the sin.[3]

Second, as we speak the truth in an *affirming* way we make an emotional deposit in the person we're trying to help. All of us have an almost unquenchable thirst for affirmation. The more we hear the positive truth about ourselves, the more we are boosted up.

Also, the truth usually needs to be proclaimed to a wounded person over and over. Some people who've been deeply wounded and believed lies about themselves for years will need to hear the truth about themselves repeatedly in order to keep it vividly alive in their daily lives. After she'd had her "spirit partners" exorcised, Julie needed to hear the truth about herself repeated often. After experiencing their presence for years, it took time to get used to her new freedom.

REACH UP!

After we have reached out and then reached in, we need to reach toward God to gain his perspective on others. If a group leader is be effective, he or she must begin with the compassion of Christ. The word the gospel writers continually used to describe Jesus' ministry was *compassionate*. The Latin roots of compassion come from *cum patior*, which means to join someone in his struggle, or to endure with someone.

In his book *Stranger to Self-Hatred*, Marine-turned-priest Brennan Manning says that when our hearts are filled with compassion for others there is "no room for romanticized idealism, condescending pity, or sentimental piety."[4] As we see others accurately through the eyes of Christ's compassion, we are able to walk in humility and remember that our issues aren't really so different from others'.

The supernatural capacity to see people through the eyes of

God is captured in the following story.

> I stand by the bed where a young woman lies, her face postop-
> erative, her mouth twisted in palsy, clownish. A tiny twig of the
> facial nerve, the one to the muscles of her mouth, has been sev-
> ered. She will be thus from now on. The surgeon had followed
> with religious fervor the curve of her flesh; I promise you that.
> Nevertheless, to remove the tumor in her cheek, I had to cut
> the little nerve.
>
> Her young husband is in the room. He stands on the oppo-
> site side of the bed, and together they seem to dwell in the
> evening lamplight, isolated from me, private. Who are they, I
> ask myself, he and this wry-mouth I have made, who gaze at
> and touch each other generously, greedily? The young woman
> speaks.
>
> "Will my mouth always be like this?" she asks.
>
> "Yes," I say, "it will. It is because the nerve was cut."
>
> She nods, and is silent. But the young man smiles.
>
> "I like it," he says. "It is kind of cute."
>
> All at once I know who he is. I understand, and I lower my
> gaze. One is not bold in an encounter with a deity. Unmindful,
> he bends to kiss her crooked mouth, and I so close I can see
> how he twists his own lips to accommodate to hers, to show her
> that their kiss still works.[5]

This husband gazed beyond the scars and abnormal face of his
wife and saw something wonderful because he looked with the
eyes of God. He possessed the rare but necessary skill we need if
we are to be useful to God—to be able to see beneath the wreck-
age of people's lives to their priceless value as human beings.

Pair and Share Questions

1. What could your group do right now to reach out and make a difference in the neighborhood where God has assigned you?

2. What is the greatest challenge to working with troubled people in your group?

3. If you do not currently belong to a small group, what can you do to research your options?

4. If you are currently a member of a small group, describe the changes that have taken place in your life because of the group.

5. Consider becoming an outreach advocate for your small group. Take the initiative to plan and promote servant warfare projects for your group.

6. In your church, can you identify a functioning triage unit? Describe its strengths and weaknesses.

7. How well are your current layleaders equipped to handle the hurting people in their groups? What types of training might enhance their skills?

SEEING CLEARLY
IN THE TRENCHES

Victory belongs to the most persevering.
— Napoleon —

One Monday a few years back I was particularly depressed. Pastoral work is always rigorous, but for some years, due to facility constraints, I have spoken at six services each weekend. Despite the fact that many people have come to know Christ every Sunday, this particular Monday I was unable to see a single thing God was accomplishing. I concluded that my ministry wasn't going to make a difference in anyone's life. The only thing I knew to do was make an announcement to my wife: "I'm quitting the ministry! And this time I mean it." Janie had heard this kind of talk from me before. She used to get a bit concerned when I threatened to pull out of pastoring, but this time she was impassive as she asked, "So what are you going to do now that you're not pastoring?"

"Oh, I don't know. Maybe I'll sell cars or something."

The skeptical look on her face told the whole story. She suggested, "Why don't you go for a drive and think things through? Usually that helps when you're stressed out. And while you're out, could you be a sweetheart and pick me up a burrito?"

I walked out of the house thinking, "No one understands me."

I took her advice and drove around for an hour or so while I complained to the Lord about what he wasn't doing in my ministry. As I pulled into the fast-food drive-through and waited for the burrito, I sensed the Lord speaking to me. Don't get me wrong—I didn't hear an audible voice speaking out of the sky, nor did he talk to me through the drive-through speaker. Rather, in a subtle, quiet way I sensed the Lord impressing something on my heart. *"If you will open your door I will give you a gift!"*

I felt a little silly, but I figured I had nothing to lose, so I opened my car door and looked down. There directly under me, embedded in the asphalt, was a tarnished penny. At first I thought it was a piece of gum because it was so flat and dark. I reached down to pry out the coin and held it in my hand feeling less than thankful for this "gift." The Lord spoke to me again: "Many people in this city feel about as valuable as discarded pennies. I've given you the gift of gathering people who seem valueless. Though these are the people that the world casts off, they have great value to me. If you will open your heart, I will bring you more pennies than you know what to do with."

◆◆◆

"If you will open your door I will give you a gift!"

◆◆◆

I was deeply touched by all of this and arrived at the drive-through window with tears in my eyes. Knowing that God was involved in all I was doing relieved my frustrations.

As I look back on the penny incident, it all makes sense to me. My life and ministry had been doing major damage to the kingdom of darkness as people regularly came to Christ. Broken believers were being restored to emotional and spiritual wholeness. Others were committing themselves to discipleship. Obviously this sort of activity is not popular with the powers of darkness, so I came under attack. In my naiveté I used to picture spiritual assault in a cartoonish way, with demons causing odd calamities, or maybe even Satan himself attacking me. But that simply isn't the way it works.

That Monday I was discouraged, but my problem wasn't so much emotional as perceptual. I suffered from a problem common to anyone who has done servant warfare. I was perceptually impaired and began to reason, "Why try? My part doesn't make any difference anyway."

If we are engaged in spiritual warfare, we will at times experience a spiritual blindness that keeps us from seeing the great things God is accomplishing through our lives. Spiritual warfare would be far easier if we were fighting a pitch-forked guy in a red suit doing nasty things. Unfortunately we're dealing with very subtle forces that are difficult to detect. The enemy's strategy is not to engage us in direct conflict, but to do all he possibly can to wear us down until we're ready to throw in the towel in utter frustration. Ironically, as God begins to use our lives to drive out darkness in powerful ways, it's common for discouragement to set in and for us to want to quit.

◆◆◆

Virtually everyone who ever served in God's army had to repeatedly face the desire to leave his post.

◆◆◆

A quick scan of major biblical characters makes it clear that virtually everyone who ever served in God's army had to repeatedly face the desire to leave his post. Joshua threatened to bail out when he said, "If only we had been content to stay on the other side of the Jordan!" (Jos 7:7). David constantly expressed impatience as he cried out, "How long, O Lord?" (see Psalms 13, 74, 79, 89). Isaiah was despairing at seemingly slow results when he asked, "Who has believed our message and to whom has the arm of the Lord been revealed?" (Is 53:1). The apostles also got discouraged. They had fully devoted themselves to extending God's kingdom and in the end Jesus was leaving them. They must have been thinking, "For years we have followed Jesus by doing what he did and speaking his words to the world, and where has it gotten us? We're down to eleven disciples, and now Jesus is taking off."

These pillars of the church were facing their greatest spiritual battle to date: to fend off the desire to resign almost before they got started. When Peter said, "I'm going out to fish" (Jn 21:3), I don't believe it was an innocent suggestion that they take a break and fish a little. I believe Peter meant, "I want to return to fishing as a vocation." Sometimes we suffer through periods of discouragement that run so deep we simply throw up our hands and say, "My life isn't making a difference, so why try?"

◆◆◆

Unless these problems are corrected, they
will lead to frustration, and ultimately
to an overwhelming desire to quit.

◆◆◆

Servant warfare is tough on the spiritual eyes. I have observed several different kinds of vision impairment, and those who are being used by God can be afflicted with one or more of them. Unless these problems are corrected, they will lead to frustration, and ultimately to an overwhelming desire to quit.

THE GALATIANS: TIRED-EYED SAINTS

Paul had a concern for the church he established in Galatia, much like a parent who worries about a young child being bullied at school. This city was filled with pagan, anti-Christian religion, yet the Spirit of God was moving powerfully as many found Christ

and turned from dark ways of living. I believe the Galatian believers had practiced servant warfare in their city for years as they
sought to demonstrate the fruit Paul described to them: "love, joy,
peace, patience, kindness, goodness" (Gal 5:22).

After a long period of faithfulness they became worn down,
spiritually depressed, and ready to give up. Their vision had
become impaired and they had fallen into compassion fatigue. Paul
hoped to build their courage in Galatians 6:9 when he offered this
admonition, "Let us not become weary in doing good, for *at the
proper time we will reap a harvest* if we do not give up." The apostle saw that if the Galatians could gain a perspective beyond their
present suffering, they would be able to endure.

Anyone who hopes to be effective in servant warfare must learn
to look beyond the frustration of the present. What are some ways
we can see beyond the here and now and avoid becoming "weary
in doing good" as we practice servant warfare?

Expect joy. After some time in the church world some Christians
conclude that if one wants to be serious about Christ, one must go
about life with a somber attitude. Too often we develop the perspective of a straight-faced pastor friend of mine from Oslo who
says, "Steve, in Norway Christians are very serious about joy!"

I don't know where we get the notion that following Christ is
only for the clinically depressed, but Scripture certainly doesn't
support that view. Paul said that the mark of God's Spirit's presence is "freedom" (2 Cor 3:17). In a similar vein, Peter reminded
the suffering churches dispersed throughout the world of the
"inexpressible joy" (1 Pt 1:8) that is found in following Christ.

One lady I spoke with recently has gotten in touch with the joy
that comes as we give of ourselves in servant warfare. As a new
Christian she drew from her background when she joked after
delivering food to a single mom: "Doing this gives me more of a
rush than taking drugs ever did!" Because of her early experiences

in following the Lord, this woman has been positively conditioned over the past year to expect that the Christian life—including the element of servant warfare—is a joyous experience. We tend to see exactly what we expect in life, so why not anticipate joy?

Expect fruit. Even before "Victory Gardens" were in vogue, my grandpa had a very large garden. Though he worked ten-hour days in his vocation as a banker, his passion and therapy was working in his garden. When asked by friends how he stayed motivated to put in the long hours needed to tend his garden he said, "My secret is simple: *I always have something ready to harvest.* As long as I can see fruit coming forth, I can handle the work." Though he lived in Kansas where the winters are harsh, he planted a wide variety of crops that could be harvested almost year-round.

◆◆◆

"I always have something ready to harvest."

◆◆◆

Like my grandpa's approach to gardening, a key to staying in the fray with servant warfare projects is having enough diversity in our projects that we can regularly see the fruits of our labor. Whenever possible I prefer to sponsor several outreach projects at once—a car wash, a soft drink giveaway, and a parking meter outreach. Plan practical outreaches throughout the entire calendar year so that activities take place regularly. Harvesting fruit consistently will motivate group members to continue their efforts and keep them from getting discouraged.

Expect positive change. The Galatian Christians faced a spiritual paradox: Though God was moving strongly in their city, it seemed to them that he was doing little. Change wasn't happening fast enough to please them.

I relate to their impatience. It seems that people never change fast enough to suit me. I know from experience that if I focus my attention on specific changes I think others need to make, then I will become impatient. However, if I can see beyond appearances to the deeper work God is doing, then I can patiently endure.

Paul's encouragement to the Galatian believers was to train their eyes to see the work God was accomplishing. "What counts is a new creation," he said (Gal 6:15). God is building something significant through our lives as we serve. Instead of focusing on what doesn't appear to be happening, we need to look beneath the surface for the deeper work of God.

ELIJAH: FAR-SIGHTED PROPHET

An equally difficult perception problem is being able to see what God is doing in the long run, but being blind to what he's doing right under our noses. Those who suffer from spiritual far-sightedness are usually visionaries who can perceive the distant truths of God, but sometimes entirely miss what is obvious and imminent.

This was the problem the prophet Elijah had at Mt. Carmel (see 1 Kings 18). Elijah demonstrated an amazing capacity to see the greatness of God when he took on the 450 false prophets of Baal. To prove the power and presence of God he prayed a simple prayer and fire rained from heaven. Elijah could see the big picture better than anyone. But as the dust settled on Mt. Carmel after the firestorm, Queen Jezebel sent a threat to Elijah that frightened him so much that he ran away to the hills and asked God to kill him. His response would have seemed odd at any time in light of his popularity and spiritual power, but it is doubly odd that it occurs on the heels of the one of the greatest demonstrations of God's power in the Bible.

Though Elijah's reaction must have seemed odd to observers, he didn't recognize his folly because he couldn't see what was right in front of him. Elijah could trust God with huge cosmic show-downs, but not in the day-to-day battles. Perhaps we don't ask God to kill us like the prophet did, but we all sometimes feel alone in our work for God.

◆◆◆

We so easily shift our focus from God's great-ness and exaggerate the power of the enemy.

◆◆◆

A counterattack is common soon after a significant spiritual victory, as in the case of Jezebel's threat to Elijah. We so easily shift our focus from God's greatness and exaggerate the power of the enemy. To avoid stepping into the traps right in front of us, we must be aware of a few important truths.

Counterattack is real. When we are effective in defeating the powers of darkness through servant warfare, we shouldn't be surprised when we face spiritual resistance. As we push against evil, evil pushes back against us. Sometimes in the course of straining our eyes to pick up on the activity in the spiritual realm, we can miss the evident.

This was my experience in my first church-planting endeavor when I suffered through some severe bouts of warfare in Norway. For the first couple of months in Oslo I woke up every morning with flu-like symptoms, something that was odd for me since I am rarely ill. Then just about the time the flu symptoms subsided, I squatted down to pick up something off the ground and tore the cartilage in my knee. When I saw an orthopedic surgeon, he thought it was odd that such a severe injury had resulted from a simple squat. The one-two punch of the flu and the knee injury set me back emotionally, and I began to ask, "Why, God? Didn't you send me here to do your work?"

I now see that both my recurring flu and knee injury were probably the result of counterattack from the forces of darkness. I had moved to Oslo to start a new church that would ultimately bring people to Christ. That's not exactly good news to the enemy's hordes. Naturally they resisted my steps of obedience to God. We need to view spiritual opposition as a reality, pray against it, and keep going forward. If doors close in our faces, we need to look for the door the Lord opens next.

Darkness is limited. God is greater than any force in the universe, but Elijah forgot that. When ninety-pound Jezebel threatened him, he panicked and ran. When the reality of darkness stares us in the face, we often forget that it is limited—in power, presence, and intelligence.

This truth came home to me as I and a team prayed for freedom to come to a man who'd been afflicted with numerous evil spirits. After several hours of ministry I wasn't sure if there were any remaining unwelcome guests so I asked, "If there are any more spirits present here, I command you to identify yourselves."

The response back was, "There are no more of us here." Apparently the demons I was dealing with were IQ-impaired! Out of curiosity I asked, "How many of you 'aren't' there?"

A voice answered, "Three!" After another half-hour of prayer we had successfully rid this man of the three spirits who "weren't" there, along with a number of other unwelcome guests.

I certainly don't want to make fun of the trauma of someone who is demonized, but if we are to successfully deal with the powers of darkness it is vital we never forget that these powers are not all-knowing, nor all-powerful, and they are ultimately under the rule of God. These spirit beings, like all of creation, are limited in power. We must never forget they are always subject to the strength of God, no matter how formidable they appear.

You are forgiven. Elijah's underlying problem as he ran for the hills was that he didn't connect with God. Ironically, just after his major feat of faith, the prophet began to behave as though he was on his own and had to defend himself.

My own perspective has gotten twisted like this on occasion, in spite of great evidence that God is blessing my efforts to obey him. I've found that the consistent reason for these false notions is that I have not maintained short accounts with the Lord. When I haven't consistently spent time with God, worshipping, confessing, and thanking him, the enemy is able to exploit my fears in times of stress.

It is vital that we not only know by faith we are forgiven, but we also *feel* forgiven. Otherwise our human nature will cause us to interpret the normal disappointments of life as God's punishment. John knew of this tendency of the heart when he said, "Dear friends, if our hearts do not condemn us, we have confidence before God" (1 Jn 3:21).

◆◆◆

When I haven't consistently spent time
with God,... the enemy is able to exploit
my fears in times of stress.

◆◆◆

After speaking at numerous services one Sunday morning, I walked quite a distance down the street to my car, only to discover I'd left my keys back in the locked church building. In my frustration I threw my hands up in the air and asked aloud, "God, what have I done?" I sensed him speaking to my heart, "You've misplaced your keys!"

When we let our accounts with God run low, we begin to conclude that any hardships we endure are God's punishment for some failure on our part. To have spiritual stamina, we need to recognize that the Lord is with us just because he loves us, not because we behave perfectly.

PAUL: APOSTLE WITH TUNNEL VISION

Sometimes as we're involved in servant warfare we will suffer an impairment that prevents us from seeing the entire field of vision. In the spiritual realm this tunnel vision causes us to see difficulties keenly, while remaining oblivious to what is positive. It seems this was Paul's problem on occasion. "I face daily the pressure of my concern for all the churches," he said (2 Cor 11:28). Large numbers of new believers were coming into the kingdom daily, churches were springing up all over the world, yet sometimes Paul saw only the "concerns."

I was struck with tunnel vision that depressing Monday. That year my congregation had grown by several hundred members, and we'd sponsored five new church plants in the area; but all I could see were the faces of my critics, and I couldn't remember a single good thing that was going on around me.

This kind of selective vision hits all of us occasionally. Left unaddressed, it will evolve into a continual defense posture that will wear us down and burn us out. To get past this partial blindness we need to expand our field of view by looking for the small but significant things God is doing all around us. To see more than just the center of the screen we need to make an effort to see the subtle.

◆◆◆

To avoid the desire to withdraw from warfare,
we must look deeply at situations until
we see the rich work of God.

◆◆◆

Perhaps you've seen the 3-D posters that have become popular in recent years. These seem like nothing but a blur at first, but after looking at them for awhile, a hidden picture jumps out at us. To avoid the desire to withdraw from warfare, we must look deeply at situations until we see the rich work of God.

Look for what God is providing. When we are stuck in tunnel vision it feels like we're alone against the world; yet that perspective is far from biblical. Jesus promised the apostles that when they stood before critics they needn't sweat it, because they would receive inspired thoughts from the Lord on the spot (see Acts 2:4-8). The question isn't whether God *will* provide for us, but in *what form* his provision will come. Like the apostles, I have found that God's provision usually comes in the form of inspired thoughts. The only challenge is to keep my spiritual eyes open to notice these ideas as he provides them.

A friend of mine practices servant warfare with a twist on college campuses across the country. He provides students with coffee drinks and friendly debate over biblical topics. Recently a student challenged him as she shared her unique perspectives on Scripture. He had been speaking on the authority of Scripture that evening, and she posed her question in today's youth lingo: "OK, like, I think the Bible was brought to earth by UFOs. OK, so, like, what do you think about that?" His first thought was, "What a goofy way to view life!" He'd been taking it on the chin all night with questions that tested his knowledge of apologetics. Instead of responding out of frustration, however, he went with the first thing that came to mind. He answered in her lingo with, "OK, like, let's say UFOs did bring the Bible to earth. If they went to all the trouble of bringing it from a distant galaxy, OK, like, don't you think we ought to at least *read* it?" She couldn't resist his reasoning so she answered, "Well, like OK, I guess I'll start reading it."

God provides the insight we need to handle any challenge, but we must be perceptive enough to receive it.

Look for what God is blessing. Sometimes we push harder and harder against what we think is a door, only to find out it's really a wall, and the door is three feet to the left. The struggle I was having with depression was a result of our success at doing servant warfare in our city. Darkness was being bound and many were coming to Christ as a result of our serving, and now so many were showing up that we were desperate for more space and more help. I'd been looking into our options for a larger facility to accommodate our growing congregation, but money and land weren't being provided. We needed more leaders to give pastoral care to the many new Christians. It was clear, however, that God wasn't providing for our needs in a conventional way. So what was I to do to survive in the present?

Regardless of my frustrations, there were at least two things God was clearly blessing in our midst. First, our multiple service options were working well. Why couldn't we continue to expand the number of services per weekend? Eventually we offered eight weekly services and grew by 600 percent after we thought we were full. Second, God gave me the idea of expanding our group options from just one type of group to many. We had plenty of leaders come forward when we expanded our offerings to include recovery, training, practical ministry, prayer, sports, men's, women's, and singles groups. Since then we've had a steady stream of layleaders, and now a much larger percentage of our congregation is involved in groups.

Look for what God has timed. There are two words in the Greek New Testament for the English word *time*. The first, *chronos*, is quantitative time as we count it in hours, days, weeks, and years. But the second word, *kairos*, or qualitative time that God arranges, is far more important to us. If we see only the *chronos* we miss the timing and provision of the Lord and are destined to grow increasingly frustrated with what isn't happening for us. When we adopt the *kairos* perspective on time, life is fruitful and exciting.[1]

An example of a *kairos* opportunity is the window for evangelism that opened in America during the late 1960s and early

1970s. During the Vietnam era millions began to seek spiritual answers to the questions they were asking of life. I believe the Holy Spirit used the high levels of anxiety that typified that time and turned it into a *kairos* opportunity for hundreds of thousands to find Christ.

I believe that today a *kairos* of a different sort is happening in our culture. As I have shown throughout this book, as Christians encounter unbelievers through small, practical deeds of kindness, darkened hearts open to God. I don't know how long this openness will continue, but I intend to keep serving while the window of opportunity is open.

◆◆◆

We must be willing to ignore tradition
and ask, "What is God doing?" and,
*"What is God **not** doing?"*

◆◆◆

Open doors also exist on a small scale in all of our lives day to day, though they aren't always obvious to us. If we hope to walk through the doors God has open for us, we must be willing to ignore our tradition and honestly ask, "What is God doing?" and, "What is God *not* doing?"

Some Salvation Army ministers have been asking those questions in hopes of more effectively reaching rebellious kids who hang out in one Los Angeles suburb. For years these ministers had tried to win kids by inviting them to gospel meetings and passing out tracts. More recently they have been using a servant warfare approach by distributing free hot chocolate, coffee, and sandwiches. They've found that it is significantly easier to walk through a door God opens than one we try to force. Once the teens receive food, they spontaneously ask plenty of questions about God—the same questions the ministers tried to force upon them for years.

TIMOTHY: FUZZY-VISIONED PASTOR

Finally, if we hope to resist despair we need to avoid a condition that is common when momentum begins to increase. Someone has said, "If the devil can't stop us, he'll stampede us!" That was apparently the problem Timothy faced as the church he pastored in Ephesus became more and more fruitful.

We aren't privy to one-on-one conversations between Paul and his understudy Timothy, but based on the letter Timothy received, apparently this young pastor had threatened to leave his pastoral post. Paul's first counsel to Timothy was "*stay there* in Ephesus!" (1 Tm 1:3, emphasis added). Timothy was young, his church was large and at least a bit unruly. He was overworked, running in three directions at once. In his frustration he gave up on any sort of strategic approach to ministry. Not surprisingly, all he could think of was, "I want to be anywhere besides Ephesus!"

When spiritual warfare occurred, Timothy's fuzzy vision prevented him from seeing that his role made any real contribution to the cause of Christ. But instead of bailing out, Timothy needed to build a simple strategy for ministering in a balanced way. In this age when Day-Timer depression runs rampant, our unrealistic pace of life will drive us to intense frustration unless we learn how to "un-fuzz" our vision.

Focus on refilling. Timothy grew despairing in part because he gave away far more ministry than he received. We are each wired uniquely, so what refreshed Timothy might not build you up; but generally we need regular doses of three elements: reading, prayer, and fellowship.

I have conditioned the people of my church to live by the adage, "Five chapters a day keeps the pastor away." In addition to reading my five chapters of Scripture, I read other books every day to stay spiritually fresh. I spend time each day praying and writing down my inner thoughts. I have never been patient enough to spend enormous amounts of time in quietness, but a couple of twenty-minute encounters with the Lord each day are realistic even for someone like me.

◆◆◆

Five chapters a day keeps the pastor away.

◆◆◆

We also get refilled by receiving encouragement from other believers. We need to be with people, and we need to take care of our physical selves. Leaders can get so busy dealing with problems that they stop interacting with people. We all initially enlist in ministry for just one reason: people. We begin ministry full of enthusiasm and amazement that God can use our simple lives to change people, but once we become fruitful we're often promoted to "higher" positions which force us to spend less time with people and more on tasks. When we shift our attention from changed lives to structure and organization, we become drained. It's crucial that we keep contact with the people in our communities, no matter what our position.

Much like doctors who go on their "rounds" to check on patients, we can have a similar role in our communities. Each week I carry out the rounds I feel specifically called to around the community. A couple of years ago, I began to notice there were certain places where I felt particularly called to invest myself as a servant warrior. In my neighborhood there are certain families I check on regularly. A local AA service office is another regular stop on my rounds. I deliver matches, clean the restrooms, and often have a cup of coffee with the folks there. Having a regular connection with these people keeps me thinking about them, praying for them, and serving them.

Focus on your unique opportunity. God provides all of us with a chance to make our lives count in reaching the world he dearly loves. The only challenge is identifying our opportunity when it comes along. Timothy's opportunity to make his life count was undoubtedly at the church in Ephesus, though the last thing he wanted to hear from Paul was, "Stay there in Ephesus." Timothy was probably dreaming of moving somewhere where he could plant a cozy church where the people would always be nice and committed with their time, energy, and money. But God had other plans: He had specifically designed an opportunity for Timothy, and it was called Ephesus.

God sends each of us unique opportunities for ministry. Often they come to us looking like darkness that is out to swallow us. If we hope to transcend the fog that drives us to despair, we must recognize opportunities that are sent from God. What we see as obstacles blocking our path are often strategic gifts from the Lord. When facing these obstacles we think, "This is going to *break* me," yet God intends to use it to *make* us.

One man that managed to recognize his divine opportunity was a British scientist named Ernest Shakelton. Shakelton was part of a twenty-eight-member crew that left England in 1914 on a six-month exploration of the South Pole. Though they timed their trip to coincide with the southern summer, they met with unseasonably cold weather and became stuck in an ice floe. Eventually the pressure of the ice lifted the boat out of the water, crushed it, and sank it. The crew went into survival mode by erecting huts from broken pieces of the boat, and began sending SOS signals. As the months passed the men grew increasingly despondent, and after six months they concluded that no one was coming for them.

During those months of waiting, Ernest Shakelton contemplated the situation. Something rose up inside him that he'd never seen before—a capacity to do whatever was necessary to survive when others' lives were on the line. That capacity was vital, because the route before him was unimaginably arduous, and most of the time he was the only one who thought a rescue was possible. Though he was a scientist by trade, and knew nothing about ocean navigation, he became the point man of a rescue operation across thousands of miles of high seas.

Shakelton and a crew of five rigged a lifeboat with a sail, rudder, and meager supplies for their journey to the whaling station on South Georgia Island. As they shoved off, their hull hit a piece of ice that punctured the boat and nearly drowned them. Not ready to give up, they plugged the hole with a marlin spike and headed out to open sea. The small crew worked in shifts, attempting to rest in wet sleeping bags with only a thin canvas cover over them. For weeks they zigzagged their way across the south Atlantic, enduring hunger, exhaustion, and unrelenting arctic winds that so chapped them that their faces bled if they so much as smiled.

When they finally reached the island they were heartbroken to realize that the whaling station was on the opposite side. Between them and civilization was a steep, rocky mountain encrusted in ice. Facing these new odds the crew wanted to give up, but Shakelton continued to lead them. He insisted they rope themselves together and go forward.

The only way to scale the mountain was to chip holes in the ice and inch their way up. After days of climbing they reached the top, but instead of being encouraged, the crew despaired as they peered down the even steeper descent toward the whaling station. On top of the rigorous angle of decline, a dense fog prevented them from even seeing which direction the station lay. The crew lost any glimmer of hope for survival, and decided to just go to sleep and let the cold kill them.

As they were preparing to die Shakelton persevered as the leader. His idea: Build a toboggan out of rope and take the fast route down the mountain. When they complained about the possibility of hurtling off a ledge, smashing into rocks, or even going in the wrong direction in the fog, Shakelton reasoned that they wanted to die, so why not get it over with in a hurry!

They assembled a makeshift sled out of canvas and coiled rope and shoved off. To the crew's amazement, Shakelton's idea not only worked, it was actually fun! After a high-speed sled ride they broke through the fog and came to a gentle stop in the snow, a short distance from the whaling docks.

Within a couple of weeks Shakelton and the rescue crew had located the rest of their comrades. In the end not a man was lost, though at many points it looked as though no one would be saved. The trip that was supposed to last six months took one and a half years.[2] Shakelton's journey to do research at the South Pole was an apparent failure, but he turned it into the greatest achievement of his life. He persevered in spite of despair, criticism, weariness, loneliness, and overwhelming circumstances.

◆◆◆

In Christ, our part always makes a difference.

◆◆◆

In our service to God we are bound to experience significant spiritual attacks. Like the Galatians, at times we grow weary in our battle. We need to train our eyes to see the fruit and change God is bringing about through us. If we're running scared like Elijah, we need to remember that while counterattack is real, darkness is limited. Like Paul, if we're focusing on what isn't happening more than on what is being blessed, we need to look at the *kairos* timing and provision of God. When we feel overwhelmed like Timothy, we need to focus on personal refilling, and on doing our assignments from God as only we can. In Christ, our part always makes a difference.

Pair and Share Questions

1. Identify the "discarded pennies" in your life. How can you, with God's help, give them value?

2. Have you ever had the desire to leave your post in God's army? What happened to convince you to leave or stay?

3. Give an example of how servant warfare has been a joyous experience for you.

4. What projects are you involved in now in your service to God? Is there enough diversity to assure a continual harvest?

5. We need to trust God in the day-to-day little things. List five ways you do this and compare lists with other group members.

6. What is God blessing in your midst? How does your understanding of *kairos* time affect your perspective on what might be happening?

7. Are you receiving the elements of refilling on a regular basis?

   - Reading
   - Prayer
   - Fellowship.

   If not, how can you change your schedule so you will get the refreshment you need?

LET'S RELEASE
THE POWER

One of the paradoxes of our time is that
we have more power than ever before,
yet we seem more powerless than ever.
— Ralph W. Sockman —

Some years ago, I received prayer from a prophetically gifted man who saw pictures when he prayed. He reported that as he prayed for me, he saw a picture in his mind's eye of me dressed as a combat soldier with bullet belts crisscrossing my chest. The picture was odd in two ways. First, instead of the belt being filled with bullets, each loop contained a stick of dynamite. Second, not a single stick of dynamite was missing. I had a lot of ammunition, but I hadn't used it yet.

As a young pastor I recognized that picture as an accurate portrayal of my life: It had consisted more of theory than practice. I'm happy to report that over the past few years I've managed to set off a few of my sticks of dynamite for the kingdom of God.

I'm no demolition expert, but I did handle dynamite in one of my summer college jobs. My boss that summer was an impatient guy we dubbed "Stormin' Norman" for his rough-and-tumble leadership. My training in the safe handling of dynamite lasted a total of five minutes. Norman said, "Sjogren, the proper handling of dynamite is not rocket science. There's just one rule to follow other than common sense: never mix the ignitors with the dynamite. You got that, Sjogren? If you get 'em mixed up, you're gonna have trouble."

◆◆◆

*I believe the majority of Christians today
are like I was: equipped to the hilt with
the finest dynamite, but reticent
about setting it off.*

◆◆◆

An ignitor is something like a firecracker that is placed inside a stick of TNT to set it off. By itself dynamite is fairly stable, but once it's combined with an ignitor, the two become incredibly powerful. I witnessed the power of dynamite combined with ignitors each day as miners blasted away walls of solid rock. It was amazing to me how just a few sticks, strategically placed, could take out ten linear feet.

When Swedish scientist Frederick Nobel invented dynamite in the 1800s he coincidentally named this new substance after a word that was originally used by Jesus to describe the Holy Spirit's power within all his followers. Jesus promised us dynamic power to make a difference in the world when he said, "You shall receive *power* when the Holy Spirit comes upon you" (Acts 1:8). The word he chose was *dunamis*, the very root of our word *dynamite*. When we received Christ at salvation we also received the Holy Spirit—the power of God that changes the world.

I believe the majority of Christians today are like I was: equipped to the hilt with the finest dynamite, but reticent about setting it off. We already have the dynamite we need; we have the power of God's Spirit. So why have we mined so little in this world? Why have we failed to set off the power that we carry with us? Perhaps we lack just one small thing: an ignitor.

IGNITOR QUESTIONS

The most powerful ignitors are simple questions. Jesus used questions as powerful agents of change in people's lives. More often than not, when someone asked him a question, Jesus responded with a question—usually one so probing that the listener probably spent the rest of his life pondering it.

As we ponder a few simple questions, something powerful is set off inside of us. As we've seen throughout this book, it is small things done with great love that change the world. The small thing of asking the right questions sets off a big thing of the Holy Spirit's power inside us. Consider these ignitor questions.

Where is the opportunity? As a dynamite carrier on my summer job, I discovered that it doesn't take a lot of dynamite to blast away a lot of rock; it just requires strategic placement. If TNT were just taped to a rock wall and exploded, nothing much would happen. But if that same stick were placed in a crack in the rock, it would blow it apart. Similarly, we need to look for the spiritual "cracks" in our city that might easily be mined for the kingdom of God. Because each city has a unique spiritual shape, there are special opportunities everywhere to make a difference.

I recently read about a group in Panama City, Florida that has discovered a unique opportunity. Panama City is the preferred spring break site of tens of thousands of college students each April. Christians in the area felt it was no accident that these students came to their city. But how would they reach these kids? As they pondered and prayed about this, they came up with the idea of a bungee jumping operation, and Bungee Mania was born. The safety cushion below the jumper is imprinted with huge letters, "GOD LOVES YOU!" The bungee operators are trained to ask each jumper, "If this cord breaks, are you ready to meet Jesus?" Last year some 120 young people came to Christ perched on the bungee tower![1]

◆◆◆

There are plenty of unique opportunities all around us if we will simply notice them.

◆◆◆

Christians in New Zealand have found a unique opportunity to reach thousands. Gisborne, New Zealand will be the first population center of the entire world to see the year 2000. Already international media are focusing their attention on this city in preparation for New Year's Eve 1999. I am helping to train over 200 pastors who are linking up for an outreach. Christians from all over New Zealand are training and planning to converge to serve their way into the hearts of the locals, the media, and the watching world.

There are plenty of unique opportunities all around us if we will simply notice them.

What is God's preferred future? Facing the future is not an option. The only question is, will it be a future God (and you) will prefer, or something far less? During an interview at a Christian radio station I was asked a great question: "What if it became normal for Christians to serve those outside the church? What would happen if all the churches in our city began to do small things with great love, just like you're talking about?"

I suppose I'll never see all the churches in my city doing servant warfare, but the question of what *could be* is intriguing. My guess is that even if only a small number of our churches focused outward, the results could be phenomenal. Last year the Vineyard directly touched over 180,000 in our city. Another fifteen churches in Cincinnati are reaching a combined additional 100,000 per year. That's a total of more than a quarter-million people each year. If projections hold true, the total number reached next year should hit 350,000.

In the wake of the interviewer's question a number of other possible scenarios came to my mind.

What if serving became a city-wide practice in the Christian community? In recent years we've seen that churches can come together to pray. What would happen if those same churches gathered and then set out to love people in practical ways?

That is precisely what Christians in Sheffield, England are doing. Ten different denominational groups have gathered, been trained in servant projects, and then gone into the city promoting each others' churches. I was with one of these groups recently and heard a physician explain the project: "We're just Christians from across the city. We aren't trying to get you to come to any of our particular churches—we just want to see you come to know Jesus Christ." One shopkeeper's response was typical of many we served: "Are you sure all of these Christian groups are working together? I've never heard of such a thing." I could almost hear this man's internal spiritual walls crumbling as we conversed. Amazing things happen when we serve and don't care who gets the credit.

What if church leaders began to serve? In a sense, all leaders are already serving, but what if they began to demonstrate humility by taking the lead in serving their cities in practical ways? I think we would quickly see the world's critical view of church leaders change for the better. I believe people would begin to respect and pay attention to our words once we earned the right to be heard.

What if Christians stopped paying attention to our fears and critics, and instead looked seriously only at what Jesus is calling us to? On a recent trip to an amusement park I counted a couple hundred of the popular T-shirts that read, "No Fear!" I like the slogan; the only problem is that everyone wearing them looked exactly the same as everyone else in the park. In much the same way, the church has the right slogans (the Bible has 366 explicit commands to "fear not"). But are we really living out those instructions?

◆◆◆

The older I get, the more my focus is turning from the fear of failure to the fear of apathy.

◆◆◆

We spend far too much time worrying about what *might* go wrong, or what *might not* happen if we take a risk. Sometimes we're in danger of being consumed by the "what mights" of life. We're like a great-aunt of mine who never had children of her own, so she treated my siblings and me like china dolls. She loved us dearly but was usually overly cautious. I can still hear her words in my mind, "If you aren't careful, you're going to poke your eye out!" She thought I was in danger of poking my eye out on an hourly basis. Believe it or not, I still have both eyes!

The older I get, the more my focus is turning from the fear of failure to the fear of apathy—not even bothering to try to make a difference.

What is my part? Whether we're considering our role as a church reaching a city, a small group reaching a neighborhood, or an individual Christian reaching our friends, we have been uniquely wired to fulfill some role that only we can fill. There is something unique inside each of us that has been placed there by God, and once it's released it will bring God's life to many. We all have a "real us" inside that God wants to leak out into our community. Sometimes the real us is surprisingly different from what others expect.

When Jamie Buckingham was a boy he caddied for his father and a family friend, Mr. Simpson, on their weekly golf outing. Though he was only an average golfer, Mr. Simpson was unaware of his limited skills. Each Monday he would saunter up to the tee and let loose with his best driving effort, only to see the ball fly seventy-five yards or so. One day, however, Mr. Simpson let loose with an amazing shot that traveled 350 yards and landed on the green. Looking a bit stunned he leaned back on his club and announced to Jamie, "Mr. Buckingham, you've just seen the *real* Mr. Simpson." The real us is inside somewhere, just waiting to escape and begin changing the world.

I have a friend, Mary, who has discovered in her mid-fifties the real her that was untapped all her life. A couple of years ago we put her on an after-service prayer team even though she told me, "I could never do something like that. Instead of praying, I think I'll just watch the purses of the other women while they pray." But before long Mary was praying with the veterans. Something wonderful happened as Mary got in touch with her unique role. The majority of those asking for prayer from Mary were looking to receive Christ!

As the "real" Mary has emerged, many have been surprised. Shy grandmother Mary isn't just being fruitful, she's successfully working with a culturally different group, leading alternative rockers to Christ. One of her converts, a twenty-year-old woman dressed in black, told me recently, "A few months ago I didn't even think about God or spiritual things, but something has been happening in my heart. I've come to know Christ through Mary."

For years Mary thought her only purpose in life was to raise a family. But now she is serving her way into the hearts of people who couldn't be more different on the outside from her. As she prays for them, listens to them, and drinks coffee with them, she melts away their resistance.

Small things done with great love will change the world. As you and I wield the weapon of kindness, God's great love will flow through our lives. We will see him show up to do the big things that only he can do.

Pair and Share Questions

1. Does the imagery of a full belt of dynamite accurately depict your life in the area of spiritual warfare? If not, what would be a more accurate picture?

2. What do you suspect the "real you" looks like? The real church?

3. What is God's preferred future for your city? Describe it as vividly as possible.

4. Look for the "spiritual cracks" in your city. What opportunities might be open for you to insert a stick of dynamite and bring about kingdom change?

5. Design your own set of "What if" questions to ponder as a group. What can you do to actively implement change?

6. What are the fears that have kept you from following God's call on your life? Are they rational or irrational?

7. God has placed inside each of us something unique that will bring his life to those around us. With the help of your group, identify giftings in each person that bring life to others.

A Practical Guide
for Starting
Servant Warfare Projects

This book is for activists who are willing to go beyond just reading and thinking about battling the powers of darkness to conquering them with simple deeds of kindness. It doesn't take a radical person to do significant works of God. Each of these servant warfare projects have worked well in our experience in Cincinnati, and other Christians from various traditions have used them effectively, so you will be able to apply these to your own setting. This list is by no means exhaustive, but hopefully some of these projects will help you launch servant warfare in your world.

The table at the beginning of each project is designed to give you a quick overview of its various costs and benefits. Five factors are rated from 1 (low) to 10 (high) to help you determine the suitability of the project for your situation. The factors are:

Challenge: How easy is this project to apply? If you're just beginning in servant warfare it would be wise to stick to the lower level challenges and work your way up the scale as you build experience and confidence.

Consequences: This refers to the level of transformation we might expect as a result of the project, to both the served and the servants.

Cost in Time: Some projects take little time to execute, but are rigorous to prepare for.

Cost in Money: Sometimes it's possible to create big results with a project without investing much capital.

Complexity: This measures the level of difficulty. I recommend you hope and plan for initial successes that will build your confidence and momentum for more complex projects up the road.

Here are the specific servant warfare projects you'll learn about in the following pages.

1. Projects to reach the *middle class:*
Door-to-Door Prayer Teams
Summer Festival Projects
Wrap it Up
Serve Cincinnati
Practical Care

2. Projects aimed at the *needy:*
Thanks for Giving!
Food Distribution
Matthew's Party
Lamb's Lunch
Big Fun Bus Outing
Homeless Bus Cafe

3. Projects aimed at *single parents:*
Single Parent Oil Change
Single Parent Home Improvement

DOOR-TO-DOOR PRAYER TEAMS

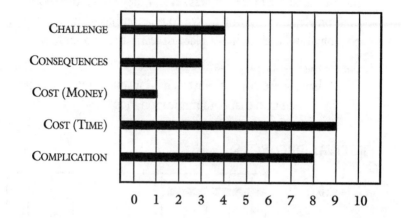

Everybody could use a little bit of prayer. Numerous surveys indicate that the average American, including the unchurched, believes in the power of prayer. The problem is that no one ever offers to pray for them.

For years teams made up mostly of women from the Vineyard have gone door to door simply to ask, "Is there anything we could pray for you about?" (We have found that women are less intimidating than men in this situation.) Usually residents are taken aback by our offer to pray for them. After all, how often has a complete stranger asked you if he or she could pray for anything? After the residents recover, they almost always come up with something to take to God in prayer.

A few other points you should consider here are:

1. Don't necessarily pray for them on the spot.
   Be sensitive. We always offer to pray for people on the spot, but we don't put any pressure on them.

2. Before you leave give them a postage-paid response card addressed to the church.
   This card provides an easy way for the ones receiving prayer not

only to report back what happened to them, but also to get them to look for more answers. When they see God respond to their prayers they may be drawn to relationship with Christ, and possibly to your church as a place to learn more about him.

3. Put them on your prayer chain.

If you have some sort of prayer chain in operation, plug them and their need into that communication loop.

FESTIVAL PROJECTS

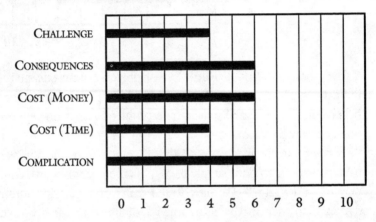

These are practical outreaches aimed at touching the thousands who attend community events. Your city probably has several summer and fall events unique to your area—perhaps a Corn, Chili, Strawberry, or Renaissance Festival. These are ideal times to touch thousands with the power of God's kindness.

If you've been to one of these festivals you probably know what sort of outreach would touch the felt need of those in attendance. For example, each Fourth of July weekend we sponsor a "Big Bang Outreach" by providing thousands of cold drinks at multiple fireworks celebrations throughout the community. Some events along these lines can be so large they require significant pre-planning. Each Labor Day in Cincinnati we serve a crowd of more than 500,000 at a river festival that draws folks from several states. We give each person a free drink with a card under the pull top that states, "You looked too thirsty to pass up!" The back side of the card gives pertinent information about our church. (The appendix in *Conspiracy of Kindness* contains a version of one of these cards.)

The goal of a festival project is to touch as many as possible in a short time. This project is easy for neophytes and the chicken-hearted. After all, how difficult is it to ask, "Would you like diet or regular?" Because of large crowds and the weight of coolers, we've found it's best to go into the festival site early with a loaded van. Since we don't have a license to give away soft drinks inside the festival area we wait for people to return to their cars and then serve them a drink. In organizing this outreach, the key is to choose the event that will give you the most outreach mileage. It's also wise to do a bit of inquiry into local laws on distributing beverages.

We prefer to gather the outreach participants in one location and transport them together in vans or buses to the outreach site. One of the great side benefits of a large group outreach is the fellowship that takes place before and after the event.

The cost of this project varies according to how many people you plan to reach. Be advised that drinks go quickly in large crowd settings. I wouldn't recommend coming with less than 500 sodas if you're going to a large public event. Typically a team of thirty to fifty can give away a van-load of soft drinks—sometimes up to 3,000. If finances are an issue, consider giving frozen popsicles instead. We have purchased these in bulk for as little as four cents apiece.

WRAP IT UP: HOLIDAY GIFT WRAPPING

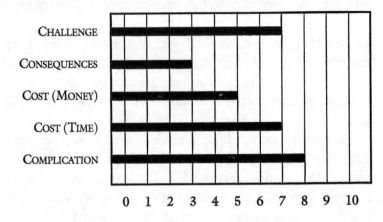

After shopping long and hard, what weary shopper could resist having their gift wrapped—for free? Several times a year we offer free gift wrapping services to shoppers at local malls. Because we focus on high-volume shopping days—Mother's Day, Father's Day, Midnight Madness sales, Valentine's Day, or Christmas—we're able to serve thousands within a short time.

This outreach can be done on a very limited basis with just a one-time, several-hour commitment, or it can be a major under-taking like the Wrap It Up project we sponsor at a local mall for thirty days straight. In a large mall as many as 500 volunteers may be needed. I recommend you start small with a one-table outreach for part of a day during the Christmas season.

The expense can be very high, depending on the quality of your supplies. In several cases churches have received underwriting by either the merchants benefiting from the wrapping or local busi-nessmen who want to make a contribution to the community at Christmas. For our first Wrap It Up projects we purchased all the supplies, including paper, bows, boxes, scissors, and tape dis-pensers. As we gained credibility, however, the malls began to assist with the bulk of the expense which can run as high as $8,000. It's nice to work into your budget free candy or cookies for patrons while they wait for the wrappers to finish.

You'll need adequate space to work. The mall we service furnishes us an empty store (approximately 20' x 40') which works well for up to twenty wrappers at a time. If the only available area is a table in a store, at least try to get one that is counter-top height to prevent back fatigue. You'll find it easier to recruit wrappers if you provide some sort of child-care space as well as a nearby restroom.

Successful recruiting is crucial for a wrapping project. It's a good idea to have small groups commit to a time slot each week throughout the holiday season. Once they are signed up, a designated caller will need to remind folks of their commitment. It's easy to forget these schedules in the rush of the holidays.

Wrappers talk with mall shoppers who are usually thrilled to have their gifts wrapped for free. We pass out a flyer at the wrapping stations that explains why we're providing the free service. We've had many people return year after year and tell us how much our service has meant to them, especially during the commercialized holiday season. One woman I spoke with had her gifts wrapped one season, came to Christ the following year, and then brought her entire newly converted family to volunteer at the next year's Wrap It Up! The kindness extended to her at the gift wrap was the final "tilt" on her journey toward Christ.

SERVE CINCINNATI

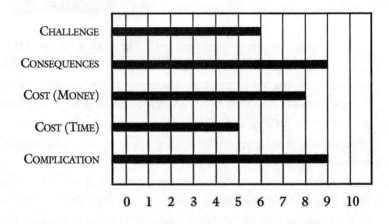

Approximately four times a years we challenge our entire church to serve in one of a variety of ways throughout a weekend. The first objective for this event is to involve as many people as possible in practical outreach projects. It is far easier to get newcomers involved in large projects with friends and family than to send them out to serve alone! There is courage in numbers. The second goal is to touch many people in the community.

We have never succeeded in involving more than about half of our weekend attendees in one of these outreaches. At a recent Serve Cincinnati about 1,500 participated—about half of our 3,000 members. But that's 1,500 that wouldn't have served if we hadn't challenged them! We involve everyone we can in reaching out, from children to teens to adults from every walk of life. (For a list of possible children's projects, consult the appendix in *Conspiracy of Kindness.*)

We build our Serve Cincinnati weekends around two or three major projects that allow several hundred people to work together. Around those we offer lots of smaller opportunities that appeal to families and small groups. Some who can't do a project on the weekend bring supplies home and do projects together during the week. For example, we have a "Parking Meter Kit" consisting of a stack of our parking meter cards[1] and a roll of dimes. Many businesspeople who work downtown take these kits to work with them and serve during their Monday lunch break by feeding expired meters in the name of Jesus.

A Serve weekend is challenging organizationally and financially if you've never done serving projects before. Therefore, I recommend you try a small-scale version of a Serve Cincinnati weekend before you unleash it on your entire church. You will no doubt work out many of the bugs connected with arranging for materials, securing permission to do projects, and communication among your project leaders. For a successful large outreach like this you'll need to strongly publicize it to your congregation and distribute a list of the serving opportunities available with times and meeting places at least a week in advance. People need time to plan and consider which project suits them best.

The day of the event, provide an abundance of maps to all activity locations. Prepare a schedule of events with as much information as possible (time, location, transportation available). You'll have a lot of questions coming in so it's wise to establish a contact person at the church during the week of the event to answer questions and deal with supply purchasing issues.

The cost of a weekend outreach is determined by the specific projects you select. Often the most effective projects that require the least skill, such as soft drink giveaways, are the most expensive. Other projects, like free car washes, can effectively involve a large number of people with little expense. Two hundred people can wash over 300 cars in a couple of hours for very little cost. A free car wash can also be effective with only ten workers. My advice is to determine how much you have to spend and which people you want to serve, then narrow your list down to a handful of projects. If your church doesn't have an established outreach budget, small groups can fund their own projects.

The projects can take anywhere from one to three hours to complete, but ideally they shouldn't last for more than two hours. After two hours the fun factor diminishes greatly and the projects just seem like a lot of work.

We like to provide an opportunity for fellowship and feedback at the end of the Serve Cincinnati outreach, so we hold a cookout on Sunday evening for all outreach participants. This is a great chance to thank leaders and participants as well as hear some encouraging stories.

Last but not least, we have found it essential to have pastors participate in Serve Cincinnati projects. Members of a congregation will be far more receptive to a message of "come with me" than "go there" and serve. Pastors will gain credibility within the church as they participate in serving others.

My long-term goal is to so condition the members of my church to the value of reaching out that they will eventually serve every day without a scheduled outreach. To encourage that mentality we have built cabinets in our church lobby to hold supplies for outreach. Whether it is a Serve Cincinnati day or not, anyone can stop by these cabinets after a service and pick up a variety of outreach kits to take with them during the week. The kits come with complete instructions for doing the project at hand.

PRACTICAL CARE

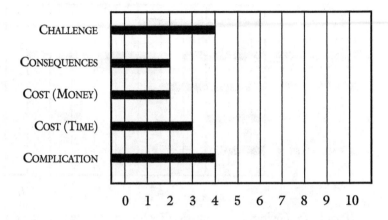

Practical Care is a program developed to match people who have stuff with people who need stuff. This ministry benefits mostly those already in the church, but we also receive from our members a regular flow of requests to help neighbors or colleagues.

To match the haves with the have-nots, a simple form is needed to capture information. This form is made readily available at our entrance so that when it is completed, the information can be dropped into the offering bag or mailed into the church office. The coordinator compiles the information in a database which is then printed and made available to the congregation. The listing contains the items and a phone number.

It is wise to launch this ministry with clear parameters regarding what you can provide and what you can't. For example, at this time we do not provide transportation, though we receive a lot of requests for this service. We do not guarantee that a particular item will be available, nor that the condition of received goods will be excellent.

THANKS FOR GIVING!

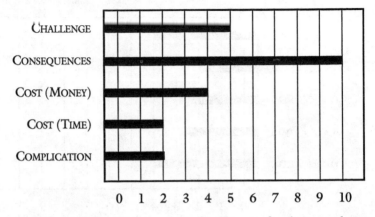

Thanks for Giving! is an opportunity for one family to reach out to another in need by providing a Thanksgiving dinner with all the trimmings. The church family works together to see that their neighbors have the blessings of a holiday meal. Those who purchase, those who deliver, and those who receive experience Thanksgiving in a new way. Last Thanksgiving we handed out dinners to 400 families—and it's easier to do than you might think.

About a month before Thanksgiving we begin to collect names of families in need. Once we have a general idea of how many families we'll be serving, we put together grocery shopping lists and ask weekend attendees to purchase food and return filled bags by a designated date. The church purchases the turkeys, which are added to the bag before delivery. (Be careful not to pick up turkeys too early, as they will start to defrost.) The Sunday before Thanksgiving, the majority of the bags are delivered either by families, small groups, or Sunday School classes.

This holiday project requires relatively little planning. We have attempted to get turkey donations from individuals with some success, but we've found that some businesses in the community are very willing to donate money to purchase the turkeys. Since individuals and families provide the majority of the food, the main expense for the church is the turkeys.

FOOD DISTRIBUTION

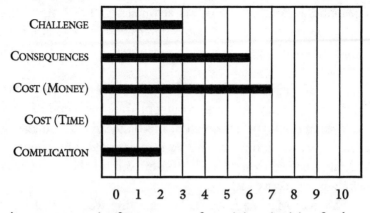

A great entry point for servant warfare ministry is giving food to the needy. We provide food in three ways:

1. Emergency Food Pantry
2. "Deliver Me" Bags
3. Single Mom's Food Delivery

A **food pantry** operation can be a established with relatively little investment of space or money. Our pantry operates out of an old farmhouse located on our church property, but you could use any room in your current church building or even a rented space like we did at one time. For years we have operated this free store several days a week by offering groceries and clothing to both the unemployed and underemployed as they seek to make ends meet. It is advertised by word of mouth only. We staff this with volunteers only. We look for those with both mercy and prayer gifts, because we want to always offer prayer in addition to the physical help we offer.

When first organizing the pantry we had to become licensed by the state to handle food for distribution. We receive some free food in the form of government commodities. (One catch to consider: There is a significant amount of paperwork if you receive any government help.) Other inexpensive food is available in most cities through membership in a food co-op (these typically sell large quantities of food by the pound at wholesale prices). Apart from these sources, most of our food is purchased from a local supplier. We buy generic brands in large quantities so we receive great prices.

An easy addition to your pantry is some sort of clothing collection and giveaway. A word of caution: You'll be surprised at the volume of clothes people drop off. I recommend that you establish one or two drop-off sites. We have constructed a huge outdoor metal structure to serve as a drop-off site for the mountain of clothing we receive each week.

"Deliver Me" bags are packed and displayed on shelving by exits for weekend attendees to take and distribute. You may want to give those you serve a card that is punched each month when they pick up their bag in order to cut down on fraud. A map to the home of a needy family who has called for groceries is attached to the bag. "Deliver Me" bags are also available for anyone in the church to deliver to needy people they know. The average cost of these bags is $8, and each provides one person with food for three to four days.

We have volunteer bag packers who spend three half-days a week sorting the clothes, packing bags, running the pantry, and praying for the customers. "Unloaders" come every other week to empty the semi truck filled with canned goods. To make this task fun we provide them with a home-cooked breakfast after their work.

Since we genuinely desire to give people tools to escape the poverty cycle, we may require the people we help for extended periods of time to attend classes in nutrition, finances, or budgeting. Those receiving services are also given opportunities to volunteer in serving projects.

MATTHEW'S PARTY

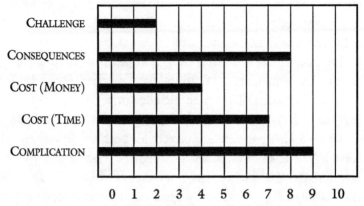

When the Apostle Matthew came to Christ he celebrated the new life he'd found by holding a spontaneous party for his friends who had not yet found Christ. The Vineyard holds a similar celebration we call a Matthew's Party by inviting hundreds of low-income residents from a needy neighborhood to an old-fashioned cookout to demonstrate God's love freely given. With a lot of imagination, some careful organization, and about sixty enthusiastic volunteers, you can throw a party that will touch hundreds of families living in poverty.

A Matthew's Party can be as simple or complicated as you wish. In addition to food and festivities (games, clowns, face painting, helium balloons, music, and food) we also usually provide a large-scale serving project to the neighborhood. This could include painting, weed removal, playground cleanup, replacing playground equipment, or whatever the local residents think is important. As an added feature, sometimes we bring in Christians who are well-known local college or professional athletes.

There is a spiritual dimension to these block parties that is mostly spontaneous, but we also look for opportunities to talk and pray with residents about specific needs. It is common for many folks at Matthew's Parties to receive Christ.

Our church covers the entire cost of a Matthew's Party unless we find local businesses to contribute supplies, prizes, or food. A wise investment might be an industrial-sized grill that will be used at future parties and for other church events.

Time commitment for the average worker is three to five hours on the day of the party. (We throw parties from 1:00 to 4:00 on Sunday afternoons. That time includes orientation, travel time, party time, and cleanup). A set-up team precedes the party team.

This is a high-consequence project for both the servers and the served. The level of complexity is high because of the planning involved and the need for large numbers of volunteers. Don't let the challenge stop you. This is a great opportunity to develop hundreds of new servant leaders as well as give small-group members something to focus on beyond themselves. A hidden benefit of this outreach is that participants come away with increased courage to reach out in other settings.

LAMB'S LUNCH

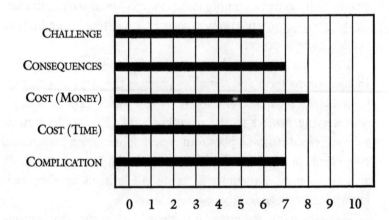

A Lamb's Lunch is a hot, sit-down meal for the homeless that is held at an urban mission or open park. A pleasant presentation of food is one way to show that we care for homeless people, restore the faith and dignity of these individuals. On some occasions we hold a Lamb's Lunch for the elderly in a fixed-income housing project.

As relationships develop it becomes natural for us to recognize and celebrate people's birthdays during the month. A cake and a small gift is a small investment to us, but makes a world of difference to a homeless or elderly person.

To publicize the lunches, we distribute several hundred invitations a few days in advance in the neighborhood we're serving. It helps to place posters in the windows of businesses to advertise the free meal.

Preparation for a Lamb's Lunch is moderately complicated, but the actual event is a fairly low risk for participants. The food costs vary depending on the deals you can find. Make your food offerings uncomplicated. In the summer serve sandwiches, fruit, cookies, and a drink. In colder months serve a hearty meal like chili or spaghetti. Our cost varies from one to three dollars per person served. The time investment, including travel time, is about three hours. Since this is a large outreach and parking lots are usually limited in the facilities we use, it helps to provide transportation for the volunteers. Traveling together to and from the event is also a great way for folks to share their adventures in serving.

I recommend you begin by linking up with a group that is already serving the needy in your area effectively and offer to come alongside to help. For example, you could offer to bring in one meal each month to ease their workload. Their credibility will help you, and they'll appreciate the energy you bring.

You'll need to recruit workers for the following tasks: cooking, prayer, serving, and greeting. All workers will need to be briefed a bit on the plight of the homeless. For example, most who have never conversed with homeless people are unaware of the diversity that exists in this group. Some are completely normal folks, while others are completely irrational, anti-social, or even psychotic. A patient attitude and friendly smile generally work extremely well with everyone.

We bring a small sound system with us to address the crowd and play soft instrumental worship music to create an atmosphere that contrasts with the sounds of the city. We usually resist the temptation to preach at those gathered. Usually they've been hammered so many times with the gospel message that they tend to view a free meal as their reward for listening to the pre-meal preaching. When we don't preach we get their attention even more than if we did, and they often open up and ask questions about the Lord.

The fairly timid will find it a reasonable risk to simply cook or clean up after the dinner. The challenge for volunteers increases as they sit with the guests at the dinner table. The highly courageous can serve on a prayer team in designated areas of the facility or park for those who need healing, encouragement, or just someone to talk to.

BIG FUN BUS OUTINGS

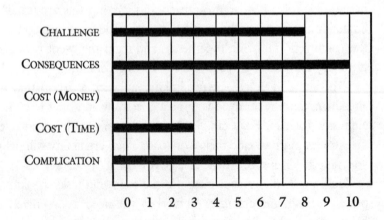

A Big Fun Bus Outing provides an easy introduction to ministering to the poor. We drive a modified bus with seats that have been replaced with shelves for bags of food and racks for clothes.

We pull the bus into an impoverished neighborhood and set up loudspeakers that play Christian music to create a positive atmosphere. Teams of two or more deliver the food and clothes to people's apartments and ask if they would like prayer.

Because of the large volume of food given away, advanced ordering and packing are a must. We often make packing the bags part of the fun by setting up an assembly line in the church parking lot or lobby. Food is purchased from the same supplier that grocery stores use. We typically pack about 150 bags per neighborhood (the maximum our bus can carry). The cost per bag is approximately $8. The modified bus we use for deliveries will carry only twelve people so a few vans or a caravan of cars are necessary to transport the volunteers.

When we pray before leaving a neighborhood, often the grocery recipients join with us and thank God for what we're doing. We follow up each Bus Outing with a postcard inviting volunteers to the next few scheduled outreaches. It's great fun to go out together afterward and share stories of how God showed up.

HOMELESS BUS CAFE

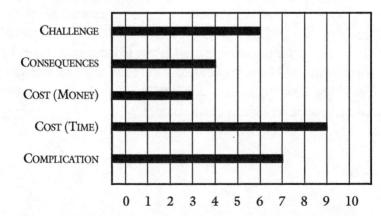

We have purchased a used school bus and replaced the seats to create the look and ambience of a cafe. On Saturday nights teams of ten to twenty volunteers man this roving coffeehouse as it parks in front of homeless shelters around the city. In addition to supplying the residents with coffee, hot chocolate, conversation, and prayer, we offer clothes, fresh underwear, and toiletries to the mostly male population. A common policy of homeless shelters is that residents cannot take a shower unless they have a change of underwear, so they get a shower at least every week or so when we stop by.

This outreach is not for the uninitiated who have never been around the needy. Not all inner-city areas are necessarily dangerous for ministry at night, but precautions and practical wisdom need to be observed. This outreach might be ideal as a second or third step following experience with a Matthew's Party or Lamb's Lunch.

The cost of building a cafe ministry bus is two to three thousand dollars. A hidden cost to consider with ministry buses is the inevitable mechanical repairs and maintenance they require. We spend an average of $1,000 a year on repairs, so buying a well-maintained bus to begin with is a big plus. When licensing your bus consider registering it as a truck instead of a church bus. With increasingly stringent state laws, a truck is usually far easier to register, inspect, and insure. A note for the codependent: Resist the desire to offer to drive homeless people to your suburban church. They may ask for this favor, but unless you feel specifically called by God to this and have the resources and time available, I recommend you direct them to quality local churches that are probably far better at pastoring them than you or I.

SINGLE PARENT OIL CHANGE

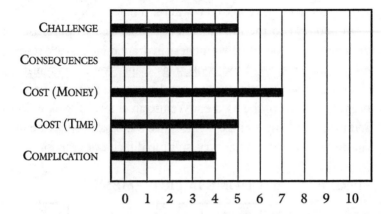

Approximately once a month we sponsor a free oil and filter change for the automobiles of single parents, the elderly, and the unemployed. Most of those we help are from our church, but a growing number are not connected with our church. These people depend on an operational vehicle, but they lack the time and money needed to maintain their cars, taxing their already tapped-out lives. By performing this simple task for these overburdened people, we make their lives a little easier and we show them the love of God in a profound way.

We announce in our bulletin an upcoming oil change a couple of weeks in advance. We require them to sign up in advance. This is important so that the correct oil filters can be purchased for people's cars. We mail a reminder a week before the actual oil change. We usually do the work on Sundays after services, scheduling the cars in fifteen-minute time slots. With teams of twelve to fifteen volunteers we can work on as many as five cars at a time.

Volunteers needn't be professional mechanics, just willing learners. After visual inspection of tires, lights, windshield wipers, engine belts, hoses, and air filters, written reports are returned to car owners to update them on the mechanical condition of their car. I recommend setting boundaries around how much service you'll provide—otherwise requests will come along for major repairs, and your mechanic crew will burn out.

In addition to the oil and filters you'll need to purchase oil drainage pans, oil filter wrenches, hydraulic jacks, jack stands, mechanics' creepers, hand tools, rags, paper towels, granular oil absorbent, essential fluids, and hand cleaners. You also need to properly dispose of the used oil. We use an empty 55-gallon drum and make recycling arrangements. Once the basic supplies are purchased, continuing the ministry isn't too difficult or expensive.

SINGLE PARENT HOME IMPROVEMENT

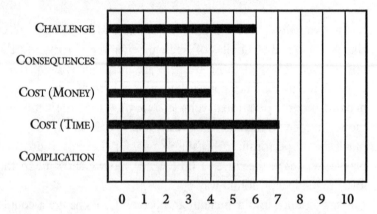

Single parents, especially moms, seem to have more things broken than working a lot of the time. For this outreach, teams of three to four somewhat skilled volunteers go to single-parent homes to do simple carpentry repairs, fix simple appliance problems, and do reasonable outside house projects such as trimming trees or cleaning out rain gutters. Before going out to do repairs, we hold a training session for the improvement-impaired. Volunteers hone repair skills and then practice them by helping those in need.

A key element to this outreach is to confine projects to what can be completed in one visit. Sometimes the work we complete has been waiting for years to be done, so we can give a significant blessing by fixing a leaky faucet, repairing a window air conditioner, or painting a room. Before we leave a home, we always offer prayer.

HOW TO CONDUCT
A SERVING SURVEY

Wherever I speak on the topic of servant warfare, the question I'm most often asked is, "How do you come up with the creative servant projects you do?" Servant warfare is based on the simple premise that as we relieve the pain or frustration of people in the name of Jesus, we will gain credibility to share Christ. Human pain and frustration are on the increase, so as servants of Christ we have great opportunity. We will never be unemployed!

I believe there are hundreds of servant warfare projects yet to be discovered. The key word is *discover*. We will best discover these new projects by following a few simple pointers.

PRAY

First pray to see those around you as God sees them. We must have the inspiration of the Holy Spirit to be effective. Servant warfare is rigorous work and occasionally is difficult to weather. Once we have seen the lost around us as God sees them, however, we will be motivated to run with endurance.

Second, in prayer make yourself available to God. He has a plan in mind to use you to redeem those around you. If we seek to hear him, I believe he will make his plan clear to us.

Third, begin to pray for the salvation of those you feel called to serve. As you pray in this way, you will naturally begin to watch for the Lord's work in their lives.

PONDER

What projects might work in your community? Ask questions along these lines:

Whom am I to serve?

How am I to serve?

Where am I to serve?

Where is their *pain*?

What do they *value*?

What do they *fear*?

Record your ponderings on paper as they come to you. Ask God to clarify your assignment. The question here is not *if*, but *what* God has for you to do. If you ask God to show you the pain of your city, he will. The problem for most of us is that we stopped looking at the pain around us a long time ago.

Once you have made yourself available, begin to pay attention to the desires in your heart. When the desire to serve someone comes to you, take note. I consider 100 percent of those thoughts and desires to be inspired by the Holy Spirit and I try to act on them. The human heart, even after Christ comes in, is terribly self-ish. Unselfish desires to serve will come more and more often as you practice being kind.

PUTTER

Puttering is a word the English use to describe going about one's day with a carefree attitude. It's taking a break from task-focused living in order to simply notice what you would normally miss. To putter is to watch life at a slow enough pace that you can see clearly and deeply. Start puttering around your community and keep your eyes open for the opportunities God will show you.

I am driven enough through life that I can easily go for weeks and hardly notice people. My best new project ideas come to me as I putter at a local mall with a cup of café mocha and mull over the question, "Where is there brokenness, frustration, and pain I can address?"

As Jesus looked over Jerusalem he was overwhelmed by the brokenness of the people there. "O Jerusalem, Jerusalem!", he cried out (Lk 13:34). Perhaps that same spirit was behind Paul's comment in Romans about praying in groanings too deep for words (see Romans 8:26). As you get in touch with the pain of your city, you will begin to identify new ways of serving your way into the hearts of the lost around you.

PRACTICE

We need to practice in order to find out what works well where we live. What goes over for you may be very different than what is successful in my city. We will learn what is uniquely effective only as we step out and experiment.

One project I'm practicing with a friend is cleaning out rain gutters using a high-powered leaf blower with a special attachment. After doing this a couple of times I already know I need a poncho of some sort to protect my clothes from the black stuff that lurks in gutters. I have also discovered that some gutters in ill repair are easy to blow off the side of the house!

Neighbors are great to practice on. Try approaching them with this proposition: "As a Christian I believe it's a wonderful privilege to serve. What specific project could I do for you?" Give them a few days to think about it. If they can't think of anything, offer to blow out their gutters!

PURSUE

To really make a difference in your city you will need more than just you. Pursue strategies to attract others to help you. As you are faithful to serve at regular intervals and then simply tell of your successes in the community, volunteers will show up to serve with you. If you continue to serve a couple of times or more per month for six months, you will create sufficient momentum to pursue a long-term serving ministry in your city.

PLAN

Successful servant warfare projects don't just happen. It's dishonest to say we value something if we don't plug it into our schedules. If you are already maxed out, ask God to give you a creative alternative. Perhaps you could add a serving project onto something you're already doing, such as serving hot chocolate before or after your child's soccer game on Saturday mornings.

You will have 168 hours in every week for the rest of your life. Take just one hour a week, pick a starting date, and you'll be well on your way!

RECOMMENDED READING
RELATED TO SERVANT WARFARE

Bickle, Mike. *Passion for Jesus.* Lake Mary, Fla.: Creation House, 1993.

Any veteran servant knows how easy it is to become weary at times. Mike Bickle's book gets at the root of what every servant needs: to be stimulated by great passion for God. I have been empowered by this book and have spoken with many others who have been ignited by its message.

Campolo, Tony. *The Kingdom of God Is a Party.* Dallas: Word, 1990.

Campolo believes that following Jesus is more fun than anything in the world. I agree and think you will too after reading this inspirational volume. He does a fantastic job of describing the atmosphere of God's kingdom.

Campolo, Tony. *You Can Make a Difference.* Dallas: Word, 1984.

This book is aimed at young people who have perhaps concluded that no matter how they live their lives, they will have no impact in the world. Campolo says nothing could be further from the truth. By calling the reader to several commitments, he encourages us to live out of the conviction that the life of Christ in us can change things around us.

Clinton, Robert. *The Making of a Leader.* Colorado Springs: Navpress, 1988.

This is one of the few books I reread every year. I need to be reminded of the fact that difficulties that come my direction in life and ministry are redemptive in the hands of God. Clinton shows that every leader goes through numerous predictable phases over the course of a lifetime of influence. One of the keys to effectively exerting ourselves in ministry is understanding where we are headed.

Comfort, Ray. *Hell's Best Kept Secret.* Springdale, Pa.: Whitaker, 1989.

I don't always agree with Comfort's in-your-face confrontational approach to communicating the gospel, but in the midst of emphasizing the kindness of God we can't soft-pedal the nonnegotiable truth of others' need for salvation. Comfort maintains that it's essential that those we reach out to come to understand they've broken God's law and are in need of salvation.

Curtis, Lang & Petersen. *Dates with Destiny.* Grand Rapids: Fleming H. Revell, 1991.

The authors are former editors of *Christian History* magazine. They conducted a survey among their readers regarding the top one hundred events or personalities in church history. Many of these significant figures were simply servant warriors who did one thing well.

Dawson, John. *Taking Our Cities for God.* Lake Mary, Fla.: Creation House, 1989.

Dawson sees that as we discover the historical prevailing spiritual mindsets of a city and then serve in the opposite spirit, we will tear down the prevailing powers of darkness. He offers plenty of convincing stories to back up his thesis.

Hummel, Charles. *Fire in the Fireplace.* Downers Grove, Ill.: InterVarsity Press, 1978, 1993.

This is hands down the best book on spiritual gifts available. If we are going to do ministry in the power of God's Spirit, we need to use all the gifts he has made available to us. The latest revised version offers Hummel's updated perspectives on trends in the area of gifts in the church over the past couple of decades.

Lawrence, Brother, and Frank Laubach. *Practicing His Presence.* Portland, Me.: Christian Books, 1973.

This volume is the combined efforts of two mystics who were effective at living fully in the world yet maintained intimacy with Christ. Often books on prayer are so vertical in orientation that their wisdom is difficult to translate into the day-to-day world. Not so with this one. Lawrence and Laubach inspire the reader to believe that intimacy with Christ can happen in the midst of an outwardly focused, productive life.

Manning, Brennan. *The Ragamuffin Gospel.* Portland, Ore.: Multnomah Press, 1990.

Thoughts on mercy, grace, and compassion from a Christian veteran of life. The stories motivate and inspire hope. This is a great book to capture the heart of someone who struggles to view others with God's grace.

Manning, Brennan. *A Stranger to Self-Hatred.* Denville, N.J.: Dimension Books, 1982.

Manning shows that Jesus is our model for building and maintaining healthy self-esteem.

Silvoso, Ed. *That None Should Perish.* Ventura, Calif.: Regal, 1992.

This Argentinean believes God's aim is to win everyone in our city to Christ. He conveys his experiences in trying to win entire cities in South America and the US. I like his approach because it outlines a comprehensive battle plan for taking on the spiritual powers that keep people away from salvation.

Sjogren, Steve. *Conspiracy of Kindness.* Ann Arbor, Mich.: Servant, 1993.

If the word *evangelism* frightens you then this book is for you. By making the initial contact point with non-Christians through serving, we can include the vast majority of the church in the effort instead of relying on the orally gifted. Lots of ideas for outreach projects that are based on simple acts of kindness.

Sweeten, Ping, Clippard. *Listening for Heaven's Sake.* Cincinnati: Teleios, 1993.

Simple listening is a powerful weapon for warfare as well as a healing salve for those in pain. In a society such as ours that mostly gives information, it is nearly shocking for someone to offer to really listen. This book could be used as a small-group study resource.

NOTES

TWO
Go and Change the World!

1. *Renton (Washington) Tribune News*, March 3, 1990.
2. *20/20*, ABC, April 5, 1991.
3. Scott Alexander, *Rhinoceros Success* (Laguna Hills, Calif.: The Rhino's Press, 1980).

THREE
Chasing the Right Game

1. Phone interview with Dr. Eddie Gibbs, June 13, 1995.
2. Peter Wagner, *Church Planting for a Greater Harvest* (Ventura, Calif.: Regal, 1990), 35.
3. Billy Graham speaking at the InterVarsity Missions Conference in Urbana, Illinois in December, 1976.

FOUR
Three Truths That Empower

1. Bruce Larson, used by permission.
2. D. John Richard, *Evangelical Fellowship of Asia*, New Delhi, India, July 1991.
3. J.B. Phillips, *Your God is Too Small* (New York: Macmillan, 1961).
4. Judy Tarjanyi, "Cincinnati Church Spreads the Word by Serving Everyone," *Toledo Blade* (February 1995).

FIVE
Changing Spiritual Climates

1. Ray Coleman, *Lennon: The Definitive Biography* (New York: Harper Perennial, 1992), 143.
2. *Merriam-Webster's Collegiate Dictionary*, 10th ed. (Springfield, Mass.: Merriam-Webster, 1993).

SIX
Binding the Powers of Darkness

1. David Stern, *Jewish New Testament Commentary* (Clarksville, Md.: Jewish New Testament Publications, 1992).
2. Wagner considers the Pentecostal movement that was launched in the early 1900s to be the first move of the Spirit in this century. The charismatic movement of the 1960s that affected the historical denominations is the second wave.
3. Charles Kraft, "What Kind of Encounters Do We Need in Our Christian Witness?", *Evangelical Missions Quarterly* (July 1991).

SEVEN
Renovating Minds

1. James F. Engel and Wilbert Norton, *What's Gone Wrong with the Harvest?* (Grand Rapids, Mich.: Zondervan, 1975).

EIGHT
Loving Our Neighbors to Freedom

1. Michael Hart, *The 100* (New York: Citadel, 1995), 17.
2. Hart, 21.
3. Peter H. Davids, *The New International Commentary on the New Testament, First Epistle of Peter* (Grand Rapids, Mich.: Eerdmans, 1990), 115.
4. Davids, 115.
5. "The Door Interview," *The Door*, July-August 1993, 6.

NINE
The Power of Small Groups

1. Robert Wuthnow, *Sharing the Journey* (New York: Macmillan, 1994), 45.
2. For a more thorough discussion of servant evangelism cards, see my book *Conspiracy of Kindness* (Ann Arbor, Mich.: Servant, 1993), 214.
3. For a more thorough discussion of small-group listening, rational thinking, and confrontation skills, I recommend *Listening for Heaven's Sake* by Sweeten, Ping, and Clippard (Cincinnati: Teleios, 1993).
4. Brennan Manning, *Stranger to Self-Hatred* (Denville, N.J.: Dimension, 1982), 112.
5. Richard Selzer, *Mortal Lessons* (New York: Simon & Schuster, 1974), 45-46.

TEN
Seeing Clearly in the Trenches

1. *The New International Dictionary of New Testament Theology*, Vol. 3, explains, "Chronos chiefly denotes the quantitative, linear expanse of time, a space or period of time, and is thus a formal and scientific conception of time... By contrast, the characteristic stress of kairos draws attention to the content of time, negatively as crisis and positively as opportunity. The NT understanding of time is not the formal concept of *chronos*, but that of *kairos*, qualifying the content of the time of Jesus, which stands in the foreground." p. 826.
2. For more reading on Shakelton, check out F.A. Worsley, *Shakelton's Boat Journey*, (New York: Norton, 1977), and Roland Huntford, *Shakelton*, (New York: Atheneum, 1986).

ELEVEN
Let's Release the Power!

1. *The Source*, a newsletter publication of International Christian Ministries, P.O. Box 4668, Modesto, Calif. 95352.

Appendix One
A Practical Guide for Starting Servant Warfare Projects

1. You can request a sample of this card via fax at (513) 671-2041.